Contents

YORK NOTES

General Editors: Professor A.N.Jeffares (*University of Stirling*) & Professor Suheil Bushrui (*American University of Beirut*)

John Keats

SELECTED POEMS

Notes by Charlotte Carstairs
MA (ST. ANDREWS)

 LONGMAN
YORK PRESS

YORK PRESS
Immeuble Esseily, Place Riad Solh, Beirut.

LONGMAN GROUP UK LIMITED
Longman House, Burnt Mill, Harlow,
Essex CM20 2JE, England
and Associated Companies throughout the world.

First published 1983
Fifth impression 1989

ISBN 0-582-03362-4

Produced by Longman Group (FE) Ltd
Printed in Hong Kong

Part 1

Introduction

Keats's life

John Keats was a Londoner. He was born on 31 October 1795 in Finsbury, about a mile from the Tower of London and less than half a mile from St Paul's Cathedral. His family background could be described as lower-middle-class for his grandfather on his mother's side was a small businessman, the owner of a livery stables called 'The Swan and Hoop'. Livery stables offered food and stabling for town-dwellers' horses as well as providing horses for hire; the modern equivalent might be a garage and car-hire firm. Keats's father, Thomas, worked in the stables and had married his boss's lively and attractive daughter, Frances Jennings. John was their first child, but eventually they had two more sons, George (born in 1797), Tom (born in 1799) and a daughter, Frances, known as Fanny (born in 1803). (It is confusing that Keats's mother, sister and the girl with whom he later fell in love all share the same name.)

Keats began his schooling when he was seven, at a small boarding-school in Enfield, then a village about ten miles north of London. Thanks to an exceptionally liberal and humane headmaster, John Clarke, this was a pleasant establishment where a wide range of subjects was taught (including French and Latin, but not Greek) and where beating and bullying were forbidden. As a small boy Keats showed no particular interest in literature; although he was short for his age (as an adult he was only just over five feet tall) he was a keen fighter. Both his younger brothers eventually joined him at the school and there was some talk that all three might go on to Harrow, which was then by no means as exclusive a school as it later became. However in 1804, when Keats was only eight years old, his father died after a fall from his horse and thereafter a series of family misfortunes put paid to any plans for an expensive education.

Keats once wrote, 'I scarcely remember counting upon any happiness', and in the light of his family history it is not hard to see why. After his father's death his mother very soon married again, but her second marriage was an unhappy failure; the couple separated after less than two years and it seems that Mrs Rawlings, as she now was, disappeared from the family for some time. In 1805 Keats's grandfather, John Jennings, died, leaving a sizeable estate of £13,000 (then worth a great deal more than it is now), but his will was so unclear that years of confusion over different trust funds ensued and Keats certainly felt that he never received his full due. Keats's grandmother, Mrs Jennings, took her four grandchildren to live with her at Edmonton, not far from Enfield, and managed to give them a comfortable home until her own death in 1814. There is an echo of this phase of Keats's childhood in the light-hearted doggerel verse, 'A song about Myself', written to amuse his sister Fanny when she was about fourteen:

> There was a naughty boy
> And a naughty boy was he
> He kept little fishes
> In washing tubs three
> In spite
> Of the might
> Of the maid
> Nor afraid
> Of his granny-good—
> He often would
> Hurly burly
> Get up early
> And go
> By hook or crook
> To the brook ...

But even this period of relative security was not uninterrupted. In 1809 the children's mother returned to live with the family. Keats, now aged thirteen, was delighted, and he suddenly threw himself into his schoolwork with a kind of frantic energy, refusing to stop reading even during mealtimes or when out for walks, and winning prizes for translations from French and Latin. By the time he returned home for the Christmas holidays, however, it was clear that his mother was seriously ill (probably with tuberculosis, or consumption, as it was then called). Keats insisted on nursing her himself and read aloud to her for hours at a stretch. But there was no hope of a cure and in March 1810 she died. When the news was brought to him at school Keats's grief was violent and prolonged and he hid for hours under one of the teachers' desks. In adult life Keats was extremely reticent about the early loss of his parents, but a boy whose mother dies when he is at the age of puberty is bound to be deeply affected and in particular to find his later relationships with women difficult or even painful. And it is surely possible to see in these experiences of loss and insecurity in childhood and early adolescence the sources of some of the dominant themes of Keats's poetry: the impermanence of beauty and the fragility of happiness under the constant threat of parting, illness, or death.

Keats remained at school for only a matter of months after his mother's death. In the summer of 1810, when still not fifteen years old, he left to be apprenticed to Thomas Hammond in Edmonton. Hammond was a surgeon-apothecary (that is, one who made up and sold his own medicines as well as prescribing them). Medicine, then regarded as something between a trade and a profession, would have seemed a suitable employment for a boy of Keats's background. Moreover, it is likely that Richard Abbey, the businessman appointed by Mrs Jennings as her grandchildren's guardian, wanted the boys to become self-supporting as soon as possible. During the five years that Keats spent learning to prepare pills, ointments and medicines he remained in close touch with one of his schoolfriends, Charles Cowden Clarke (1787–1877), the son of the headmaster at Enfield and himself an assistant teacher at the school. It was to Clarke that Keats owed his introduction to the great works of English literature; together they read aloud from the works of Edmund Spenser (?1552–99) and John Milton (1608–74).

Clarke remembered Keats's enthusiastic reaction to Spenser's vivid and physical imagery; 'sea-shouldering whales', a phrase from *The Faerie Queene*, particularly delighted him. At about this time Keats himself began to write poetry and the earliest surviving fragment of his verse is an 'Imitation of Spenser', an admiring attempt to reproduce Spenser's 'jewelled' language and his difficult, nine-line stanza form. In another of his early poems Keats expressed his gratitude to Clarke for introducing him to so many forms of poetry: 'the sonnet swelling loudly/Up to its climax and then dying proudly', 'the grandeur of the ode', 'the rapier-pointed epigram' and, above all, the epic, 'king' among literary forms. Keats's literary education was largely a process of self-education. Had he even been able to gain admission to a university (and his ignorance of Greek would have debarred him from Oxford and Cambridge), he would not have been able to follow a course in English Literature, for degree courses in English were not widely established in British universities until the beginning of the twentieth century. He had good reason, therefore, to be grateful to Clarke for launching him on his literary 'travels'. (See the sonnet, 'On first looking into Chapman's Homer'.)

In order to complete his medical training Keats left the village of Edmonton in the autumn of 1815 and enrolled as a student at Guy's Hospital, which was situated in 'The Borough', one of the most overcrowded, noisy and squalid districts of central London. Here he attended lectures, watched the surgeons perform operations (on fully conscious patients, for anaesthetics had not been developed), and worked as a dresser in the wards, changing bandages and cleaning wounds. At the same time Keats continued to read and write poetry with passionate enthusiasm and in 1816 his first published poem, the sonnet 'O Solitude', appeared in the May issue of the periodical, the *Examiner*. In spite of his reputation as a daydreamer Keats passed his final qualifying examination in July 1816 and would, on his twenty-first birthday, have been entitled to practise as an apothecary. However, he was becoming convinced that he must devote his life solely to poetry and he set off to spend some weeks on the Kent coast at Margate to see if solitude and a change of scene would enable him to compose some poetry worthy of his ambitions. Although the summer was not as fruitful as he had hoped, he returned to London in the autumn determined to persevere.

Keats's life as a poet was exceptionally, and some would say tragically, short. In effect it was limited to the three years from the autumn of 1816, when he announced his commitment to poetry and his abandonment of medicine to his startled and disapproving guardian, to the winter of 1819 when he was falling ill with tuberculosis. In 1820 worsening health prevented him from doing much more than revise his last collection of poems for publication, and in September that year he set out by sea for Italy, on doctors' advice, to spend the winter in the milder climate of the Mediterranean. He died in Rome on 23 February 1821, a few months after his twenty-fifth birthday, and was buried in the Protestant cemetery there. Yet in this short working life he produced thousands of lines of poetry, by no means all of it published in his lifetime. A complete modern edition fills more than five hundred pages and contains the narrative poem, over four thousand lines long, 'Endymion'; two attempts at an epic on a classical theme, 'Hyperion'; 'Otho the Great', a five-act drama in blank verse written in collaboration with his friend, Charles Brown; and numerous sonnets, verse epistles, ballads, and romantic narratives as well as the odes for which he is now most famous. This output alone would be sufficient indication of Keats's impressive energy and dedication, but he also kept up a strenuous programme of reading which included translations of the Greek epic poet Homer (ninth or tenth century BC) and of the Italian poet Dante (1265–1321), and the works of the English poets Geoffrey Chaucer (*c.* 1345–1400), William Shakespeare (1564–1616) and John Milton (1608–74). As well as Shakespeare, he read other Elizabethan and Jacobean poets and dramatists, and also the works of many living poets, especially William Wordsworth (1770–1850) whom he greatly admired.

The year after Keats died the poet Percy Bysshe Shelley (1792–1822) paid tribute to him in an elegy, 'Adonais'. But in doing so he did him a disservice, for he presented Keats as frail, hypersensitive youth who died of a broken heart, slain by the attacks of hostile reviewers. Nothing could have been more inaccurate because, until tuberculosis eroded him physically and emotionally, Keats was a robust young man, tough enough to tour the Lake District and Scotland in the summer of 1818 with his friend Charles Brown and to cover more than six hundred miles on foot, and resilient enough to shrug off the reviewers' attacks on 'Endymion' later that year. As he wrote to his publisher,

> Praise or blame has but a momentary effect on the man whose love of beauty in the abstract makes him a severe critic on his own Works. My own domestic criticism has given me pain without comparison beyond what Blackwood or the Quarterly could possibly inflict, and also when I feel I am right, no external praise can give me such a glow as my own solitary reperception and ratification of what is fine. (Letter to J.A. Hessey, 8 October 1818)

From this and the many other surviving letters that Keats wrote to his publishers, family and friends, emerges the impression of an affectionate, generous person, full of vitality and humour, who took his work, but never himself, very seriously. Even when he knew that he was dying of consumption he could make a joke about it to the girl he loved:

> ... if I were a little less selfish and more enthusiastic I should run round and surprise you with a knock at the door. I fear I am too prudent for a dying kind of Lover. Yet there is a great difference between going off in warm blood like Romeo, and making one's exit like a frog in a frost—(Letter to Fanny Brawne, probably March 1920)

Keats's collected letters have come to be regarded as a classic in their own right. Not only do they provide an almost day-to-day record of his doings, but they also offer a unique and valuable insight into the development of a poet's mind. They are essential reading for anyone wanting to come to a full understanding and appreciation of Keats's poetry; fortunately, good selections exist in reasonably priced paperback editions (see Part 5).

Keats never had a settled home. When he returned to London in the autumn of 1816 he shared lodgings with his brothers in the City, but later they moved to Hampstead, then a small country village about five miles north of the city limits. Throughout his life Keats divided his time between a sociable, wining-and-dining, card-playing, theatre-going life in London, and periodic retreats to the country for the quiet and solitude he needed to work. But Keats was not a natural solitary; isolation made him moody and depressed, and probably his ideal working conditions included a sympathetic companion, such as Benjamin Bailey (1791–1853), an Oxford student with whom he stayed in the autumn of 1817 when he was working on 'Endymion', or Charles Brown (1787–1842) whose house, Wentworth Place, in Hampstead,

Keats shared for a while in 1819 and 1820. In 1817, the year in which he was working on 'Endymion', the long narrative which he hoped would establish his reputation as a poet, he moved from Hampstead to the Isle of Wight, then to Margate, back to Hampstead, to Oxford in the autumn, and finally finished the poem while staying at the Burford Bridge inn near Dorking, Surrey. The year 1818 was similarly peripatetic; in the spring he stayed for a while in Devon, helping to look after his youngest brother, Tom, who, aged only eighteen, was already fatally ill with tuberculosis. In the summer Keats travelled to Liverpool with his newly-married brother, George, to see the couple set off for a new life in the United States of America, and then went on with Brown to the Lake District and Scotland. This was the last year in which Keats enjoyed any sort of family life, for when he returned from Scotland in August, suffering from a bad sore throat, he found that Tom's condition had deteriorated. Keats undertook the demanding task of nursing him, at the same time struggling to make headway with his latest project, the epic poem 'Hyperion'. Tom died on 1 December 1818.

Very soon after Tom's death Keats accepted Charles Brown's invitation to share his half of the house at Wentworth Place. This was what is called a semi-detached house, that is, a building designed to contain two separate dwellings of two storeys, each with its own internal staircase and front door. The house still stands, now, as then, in a pleasant garden with fruit trees and spacious lawns. (It has been turned into a museum in memory of Keats, open to the general public, and is well worth a visit.) It was here, in the spring and early summer of 1819, that Keats wrote the odes for which he is now so famous, the 'Ode to a Nightingale', 'Ode on a Grecian Urn', 'Ode on Melancholy' and the rather less highly regarded odes 'To Psyche' and 'On Indolence'.

It is likely that these months were the happiest of Keats's adult life. Sometime in the previous autumn he had met a vivacious, attractive, intelligent girl of eighteen called Frances (Fanny) Brawne (1800–65). Keats had certainly indulged in a few earlier flirtations, and there is some talk that a passing sexual escapade had left him with a mild attack of venereal disease. But Fanny Brawne was the first and only woman with whom Keats fell deeply and passionately in love. In the spring of 1819 she had become, quite literally, the girl next door, for she and her widowed mother had moved as tenants into the other half of Wentworth Place. Although she was bright and witty Fanny Brawne had no intellectual pretensions; she preferred trashy novels to serious literature and her real interests were clothes and fashion. But Keats could feel that she loved him for himself; as he wrote to her, 'I have met with women whom I really think would like to be married to a Poem and given away by a Novel' (8 July 1819).

Their period of happiness did not last long. Keats was too poor and his prospects too uncertain for him to propose marriage to Fanny although they had reached an 'understanding' (nothing as formal as an engagement) by December 1819. George Keats sent depressing news of the financial difficulties he was having in America and Keats was finding it increasingly hard to extract any sort of regular allowance from Abbey, who may even have been guilty of embezzling part of the Jennings estate. Keats was even considering looking for a job as a ship's surgeon, but set off instead in June for the Isle of Wight, in the hope of turning out some best-selling poetry that would relieve him of his desperate financial worries. Odd as this may sound, it is worth remembering that Lord Byron (1788–1824) had asked his publishers for over £2,500 for the first Canto alone of *Childe Harold* (published in 1812), and Longman had paid the poet Thomas Moore (1779–1852) over £3,000 for the romantic narrative, *Lalla Rookh* (published in 1817). Together Keats and Charles Brown worked on their tragedy, 'Otho the Great', designed as a vehicle for the famous Shakespearean actor, Edmund Kean (1789–1833). If Kean appeared as Otho in London's famous theatre in Covent Garden their fortunes would be made, but unfortunately Kean had gone to America at the time so their efforts were in vain. 'Lamia', also composed during this summer, was similarly calculated to appeal to the popular taste for exotic tales of mystery and sensation. Keats moved to Winchester and remained there until October (writing the ode 'To Autumn' in September), but the prolonged separation from Fanny Brawne was agonising. In October he moved back to London, and then to Wentworth Place, having written to Fanny: 'I cannot exist without you . . . . I should like to cast the die for Love or death—I have no Patience with any thing else—' (13 and 19 October 1819). In December, despite all the unresolved financial problems, they made some form of private commitment.

At this stage of his career, the end of 1819, the future certainly looked bleak in professional and financial terms. Keats had so far published only two books of verse. The first, a collection entitled simply, *Poems*, had appeared early in 1817 and had been neither a critical nor a commercial success. It contained seventeen sonnets, a number of verse letters, several poems with a markedly Spenserian cast, and a longer poem, 'Sleep and Poetry', in which he had struggled to formulate his poetic ideals and ambitions. In 'Endymion', published in 1818, the critics found little to praise and much to attack; they found the tale of Endymion's quest for an ideal love boring, shapeless and incomprehensible, the ideas 'incongruous', the language 'uncouth' and the subject-matter vulgar. The critic of *Blackwood's Edinburgh Magazine* called Keats 'a young Cockney rhymester' (Keats may well have spoken with a Cockney accent, for among his mis-spellings is 'sea-spry' for 'sea-spray'). But the snobbish implication of the *Blackwood's* critic was that lower-class people such as Keats should stick to 'plasters, pills and ointment-boxes' and not try to invade the aristocratic preserve of literature. Keats was relatively unruffled (see page 9), having printed his own self-criticism in the Preface to the poem. His last, and greatest, collection of poems was published in July 1820. But by this time Keats was too oppressed by illness, grief at the consequent separation from Fanny Brawne, money worries and apprehension about his enforced trip to Italy, to take much pleasure in the favourable reviews, including one by the essayist, Charles Lamb (1775–1834). Keats was so hard up that he could not have afforded the Italian journey if his publishers, Taylor and Hessey, had not made a generous contribution to the whip-round organised by his friends.

'I could not live without the love of my friends', Keats once wrote. They certainly valued and respected him as much as he appreciated their encouragement and support. Charles Brown has already been mentioned; a practical businessman with a literary bent, he was, in an un-flashy way, one of Keats's closest and staunchest friends. The young painter, Joseph Severn (1793–1879), is best remembered as Keats's companion on the journey to Italy; though emotionally not very resilient he nursed Keats through the last months of his illness and was with him when he died. John Hamilton Reynolds (1794–1852), who died an unsuccessful lawyer, was, when Keats knew him, a promising young writer with a quick, impatient intelligence. It was in correspondence with Reynolds that Keats expressed some of his profoundest thoughts on literature and its relation to human experience. Richard Woodhouse (1788–1834), legal adviser to the publishers, Taylor and Hessey, was a discreet but ardent champion of Keats's work; he often helped with the chore of fair-copying the poems for the printers and sometimes lent money to Keats out of his own pocket, disguised as advances from the publishers. Charles Dilke (1789–1864), a civil servant and co-owner with Brown of Wentworth Place, with his wife and family was generous in his hospitality to Keats. And Keats gained enormous artistic stimulus from the example of Benjamin Robert Haydon (1786–1846), a painter of tremendous energy and heroic aspirations, though very limited talent. His great achievement was to lead the campaign to persuade the British Museum to acquire the Elgin Marbles, masterpieces of Classical sculpture from the frieze of the Parthenon at Athens, for the benefit of the nation. It was Haydon who introduced Keats to the world of the visual arts, including the works of the great Renaissance painters, Titian (c. 1490–1576) and Raphael (1483–1520), that made such an impression on Keats's imagination. Keats also met the literary giants of his day, William Wordsworth (1770–1850) and Samuel Taylor Coleridge (1772–1834) as well as his close contemporary, Percy Bysshe Shelley (1792–1822), but these were acquaintances rather than friends; discussion of his relationships with them and their work will be found in the section 'Keats and the Romantic poets' (p.18).

One of Keats's outstanding characteristics as a man and a poet was his extraordinary receptiveness to experience. One aspect of this was an acute physical awareness of sensation; his poetry is full of sense-impressions, not just the effects of colour and sound, but the much more intimate and vivid evocations of smell, taste and touch. In his letters he made no secret of his pleasure in food and good wine; to Charles Dilke he described the delight of eating a ripe nectarine: 'It went down soft pulpy, slushy, oozy—all its delicious embonpoint melted down my throat like a large beatified Strawberry.' And in his letters as in his poetry his images are often strikingly physical; some Scottish peasants whom Keats and Charles Brown met on their long walking-tour in 1818 were obviously puzzled by Brown's spectacles: 'They handle his Spectacles as we do a sensitive leaf.'

This hyper-sensitivity to experience was also characteristic of Keats's reactions to human beings. Sometimes he felt so oppressed by a roomful of people that 'I am in a very little time anihilated – not only among Men; it would be the same in a Nursery of children.' But more often his reaction was an eager curiosity to know what another person's existence really felt like. In the course of their tour Keats and Brown crossed briefly to the north of Ireland and there they saw an old woman being carried along in a makeshift, kennel-like contraption slung between two poles: 'with a pipe in her mouth and looking out with a round-eyed skinny lidded, inanity—with a sort of horizontal idiotic movement of her head'. Keats's reaction was not revulsion or mockery but, 'What a thing would be a history of her Life and sensations.'

Although to begin with he was much struck by the magnificence of the Cumberland landscape, Keats eventually grew weary of picturesque views and regretted that he and Brown stayed nowhere long enough to acquire some understanding of the peasants' life. Having watched some country dancing in Cumberland he remarked, 'This is what I like better than scenery. I fear our continued moving from place to place, will prevent our becoming learned in village affairs.' The fact that some of the local girls were very pretty may have had something to do with his wish to stay in Ireby, Cumberland, a little longer, but Keats had declared elsewhere that 'Scenery is fine—but human nature is finer.' Keats himself was not religious in any orthodox sense, but in a letter to Benjamin Bailey, who was training to be a priest in the Church of England, Keats referred to religion: 'I wish I could enter into all your feelings on the subject merely for one short 10 Minutes and give you a Page or two to your liking.' Keats's capacity for imaginative sympathy with the lives of others made him, as he put it, 'ambitious of doing the world some good', and if his poetry sometimes conveys the impression of a Keats exclusively preoccupied with beauty and pleasure, the letters create an impression of a much maturer personality struggling with a vision of human life that was, essentially, tragic.

Keats and his times

When John Keats was still a child, many Englishmen of philosophical and literary inclinations were vigorously debating the significance of the French Revolution. He was too young to have his imagination fired as those of his older contemporaries, Coleridge, Hazlitt and Wordsworth, had been excited by the ideas and events in France and the rest of Europe. Yet the long war against revolutionary and Napoleonic France, which began in 1793 and ended only after the battle of Waterloo in 1815, affected Keats's England profoundly. The civilian population escaped disturbance and destruction at home, for the fighting occurred in Europe and at sea. But victory required organisation, and successive governments adapted slowly, though with eventual success, to the war effort. Moreover victory, when it came, not only strengthened the convictions of the champions of the existing social order, but also reinforced the opinions of those who had long been critical of its shortcomings. The years of peace and of Keats's maturity after 1815 saw the discussion of the 'State of the Nation' extend and deepen.

War, however, was only one powerful agent of change at the beginning of the nineteenth century. Visitors from abroad and local observers alike commented on the transformation of the English landscape and, while some were excited by what they saw, others were appalled and frightened. Much more intensive cultivation and more systematic stock-rearing could be seen in the already enclosed and increasingly well-drained and fertilised fields. The vast majority of Englishmen still lived and worked in this prospering agricultural setting, landowners and farmers were the most powerful group in the political community and the impact of good and bad harvests profoundly affected the lives and attitudes of the people. But in this landscape the development of coal mining, of the manufacture of textiles in factories and of the making of iron were bringing about the most dramatic changes for centuries. The steam engine had released an awesome new power. The agricultural and industrial developments challenged those men who wanted to explain and to justify the significance of change to their contemporaries. On his journeys to Devon, to Oxford and through the Lake District to Scotland Keats saw this changing landscape and its inhabitants and commented on them in his letters. His travels illustrate another major aspect of the economic geography of the new England: the emergence of a much-improved transport system of roads, canals and coastal sea traffic. People, produce and opinion could travel farther and faster than ever before. Stimulated by the war effort and confirmed and protected further by the long peace after victory, this rapidly changing landscape also sustained an unprecedented expansion of population.

In 1801 there were eleven million people in England. By 1821 there were fourteen and a half million. This sudden rise is still inadequately explained and its significance is widely debated. The rapid increase meant that the population was unusually young; perhaps as many as half of Keats's contemporaries were under twenty. The very low average age of the population may go some way to account for the volatile behaviour and sentimental reactions to events and ideas of the time. Young as it was, it was nevertheless a population much more closely acquainted with death than the advanced societies of the twentieth century. Some progress had been made towards eliminating bubonic plague, leprosy and scurvy and in reducing the incidence of rickets, smallpox and typhus. But infant mortality was still high and, as the Keats family knew well, tuberculosis remained a killer. To the problems of disease must be added the shortcomings of surgical and medical practice, which Keats knew from his experience at Guy's Hospital, though he would have taken for granted inadequacies that would shock us today.

This young and vastly increased population was also on the move. In the mining areas of South Wales and Yorkshire, in textile centres like Manchester, in seaports and county towns there was a growing concentration of people. They went in search of work and in the hope of self-improvement. In London Keats would have been well aware of this new development in English society. Hampstead was still a village five miles outside London, but from the height of Hampstead Heath Keats could look down and see London advancing towards him. The drift to the towns took people from one part of the country to another and some, like Keats's brother, George, ventured even further and sought a new life overseas in the United States of America. Older established patterns of life dominated by the seasons and the soil were now challenged by men whose ideas and expectations were developed in towns. This was a special ingredient in the social outlook of Keats's time; urban views and values had clearly begun to supplant rural patterns of thought and expectation.

This rapidly changing England was governed, however, through institutions and procedures that had been formed in the distant past and in quite different circumstances. English history had been remarkably undisturbed over the centuries compared with that of Europe. Its monarchy was old. But for men of liberal disposition like Keats, neither the old King George III nor his son, the Prince Regent (crowned

George IV in 1820), commanded much respect. In practice they did not govern England and neither, in any modern sense, did the Prime Minister, Lord Liverpool, and his Cabinet, most of whom were members of the House of Lords. The central government in London was strictly limited in function. It raised taxes, enforced justice, preserved order and ran the mails. Its permanent officials were few: seventeen staffed the Home Office, fourteen the Colonial Office, and thirty-six the Foreign Office. Although improving in calibre, civil servants were often men of little energy, competence or initiative. The House of Commons, which prided itself as the keystone of the English constitution, was bound by ancient procedures and conventions which limited the business it could process. Its members emerged via an antiquated electoral system which had been openly criticised for decades. Parliament assembled for only six months a year and did not begin its daily sittings until four o'clock in the afternoon. There were no organised political parties as we know them today. Central government in England was more remarkable for its capacity to survive than for any ability to reform itself or produce a legislative programme in any way appropriate to the deep changes taking place in society. Yet it found champions and challengers alike from among those who had done well out of the changes in society, the war and the expansion of England into colonies overseas.

At the local level government worked through individuals. It worked in towns and counties through an extraordinarily varied range of institutions, whose age, diversity and obscurity were in many ways their greatest strengths. Lords lieutenant, sheriffs and justices of the peace were the office-holders who provided what there was in the way of administration, justice and order in the countryside. Effectiveness depended almost entirely on the quality of individuals. In the corporate towns, many bulging with new residents, the mayor, aldermen, bailiffs and members of the common council performed their immemorial customary duties. New needs were sometimes tackled by special boards set up for specific purposes. England was a chaos of conflicting jurisdictions, and power within these local political institutions, new and old, rested in the hands of a very small group.

England differed from many parts of Europe in that it had no rigid ordering of its society, no restricted noble or clerical caste. From the wealthiest four thousand families in the population of twelve million came the members of both Houses of Parliament, the Bishops and leading clergy of the established Church of England, the officers of the army and the diplomats. Below them a group of some 300,000 with an income of between fifty and a thousand pounds per year formed the middle classes. From these families emerged the men like Keats who went into the professions: the law, the church and medicine. From these families also came the majority of those who wrote and read the periodicals and fashionable literature of the time. It was a diverse group, keen on maintaining minor distinctions. Like the population at large, all these social groups were characterised by men on the move. Wealth, talent and opportunity could carry a man swiftly upwards, and decline could happen swiftly too. The diversity of modes of government and the intricacy of the social order gave English society its unusual resilience, and meant that the rigid stratifications of some parts of Europe were unknown.

Where so much depended on the accident of personality, it is not surprising that England was a singularly disorderly and undisciplined country compared with many parts of Europe. Regency London had a very bad reputation; it was notorious for open prostitution, juvenile delinquency and theft. It swarmed with outcasts, criminals, thieves, fences, pedlars, tramps, beggars and gypsies. It was a source of fear, wonder or contempt according to the attitude of the observer. Englishmen throughout the social system preferred liberty to order. They were brutally individualistic, cruel to each other, to women, children and animals. Their favourite pastimes revealed their inclinations: all kinds of hunting, bullock-baiting, cock-fighting, quarter-staff and cudgelling, horse-racing with its attendant gambling, and boxing drew crowds from all ranks of society. The young Keats fighting at school and the mature Keats with his delight in bawdy were both very much of the time. Yet Keats reflected after seeing the poverty of Scottish peasants, 'the world is very young and in a very ignorant state—We live in a barbarous age'.

The religious element in English society did little to mitigate the roughness of the life of the majority. The Established Church of England reflected the higher echelons of society in wealth as well as in office in central and local government. The Bishops sat in the House of Lords and more than a quarter of the magistrates in the country were clergymen. The Universities of Oxford and Cambridge, as yet unreformed, were finishing schools for the wealthy and bastions of Anglican interest. In industrial areas and in the more densely populated parts of the towns and cities there were few churches and fewer clergy. Dissenting groups abounded. Baptists, Quakers, Congregationalists and the more recently developed Methodist bodies did in some measure fill gaps left by the established churches. But provision for the needy or for education was left mostly to the energy and conscience of individuals. There was no prevailing orthodoxy but in these years a strong revival of interest in morality and ethics took place, in which Christian and atheist shared a new confidence in the possibility of personal and social improvement.

This richly diversified English society revealed itself in the proliferation of periodicals, pamphlets and writing of all kinds. Without any effective control by censorship or by the central government, and carried along by the lively debate on the 'State of the Nation' and a multiplicity of issues, opinion blossomed. It is perhaps here that Keats was most closely involved in the new England, in terms of both his audience and his own inspiration.

Keats and the Romantic poets

At the end of 1816, the year in which the twenty-one year old Keats had chosen to devote himself to poetry, Wordsworth was forty-six, Coleridge forty-four, Byron twenty-eight and Shelley twenty-four. All except Shelley had well-established reputations as poets. Wordsworth and Coleridge had published their joint collection, *Lyrical Ballads*, in 1798 and the second edition with Wordsworth's Preface, a declaration of their literary philosophy, had appeared in 1800. Each had continued to publish poetry independently. A two-volume collection of Wordsworth's poems was published in 1807 and 'The Excursion', a long account of the development of a poet's mind, followed in 1814. Coleridge's 'Remorse' was published in 1813, 'Christabel' and 'Kubla Khan' in 1816. 1816 also saw the publication of the third part of Byron's semi-autobiographical narrative poem, *Childe Harold*; he had already made his name as a teller of stirring, heroic tales in exotic settings with *The Giaour* (1813) and *The Corsair* (1814). And Shelley's first substantial collection of verse, *Alastor and Other Poems*, also appeared in 1816. Keats felt, as he put it a few months later, that 'the Cliff of Poesy Towers above me', with only a handful of published poems to his credit. Six years later, in 1824, Keats, Shelley and Byron were dead, and in another ten years Coleridge, too, had died. Only Wordsworth lived on to the age of eighty, but writing virtually no poetry in the last thirty years of his life.

Some years after Wordsworth's death literary critics and historians began to see these five poets as a group or 'movement'. Using the term that had been applied to the new literary movement in France in the late eighteenth century, they called them 'Romantics', and opened the discussion that still continues of the ideas and qualities that their work had in common. It is essential to remember, however, that while these five poets lived they did not regard themselves as a group in any sense. Some, like Wordsworth and Coleridge, Byron and Shelley, knew each other well and, for a time at least, lived and worked together. Others never met, and by no means all liked or approved of the others' poetry. Keats and Byron never met each other, and although Keats admired Byron as one of the 'literary kings in our Time', Byron deplored the sentimental eroticism of 'Endymion' and called it 'piss-a-bed poetry'.

Labelling Keats 'the youngest of the second generation of English Romantic poets' makes him sound like a member of a close-knit family community, whereas Keats saw himself increasingly as an outsider, 'trying myself at lifting mental weights, as it were'. He met Wordsworth several times but although he retained a profound admiration for his work, 'The Excursion' in particular, he became progressively disillusioned with his public manner which grew more pompous, vain and dogmatic with the years. He had one or two brief encounters with Coleridge, including a memorable walk over Hampstead Heath when they discussed 'Nightingales, Poetry—on Poetical sensation—Metaphysics—Different genera and species of Dreams—Nightmare . . . Monsters—the Kraken—Mermaids' (11 April 1819). And Keats admired some aspects of Shelley's poetry but was not, on the few occasions when they met, attracted to him as a personality. After a brief, heady few months in literary circles in the autumn of 1816 and the spring of 1817 Keats became quite disenchanted with the gossip and the quarrels of this little coterie and gradually detached himself from 'that most vulgar of all crowds the literary'.

Ironically, the person who did most to drive Keats away from literary circles was the very man who had given Keats his initial introductions to John Hamilton Reynolds, to Shelley, to Benjamin Haydon, and, indirectly via Haydon, to Wordsworth. This was Leigh Hunt (1784–1859), a minor poet, man of letters and editor of the literary and political journal, the *Examiner*. Hunt performed an immensely valuable service for Keats in that, recognising his talent and his ambition, he drew him into a circle of men who believed in the value of art and literature, thus strengthening Keats's faith in himself and his future at a crucial point in his development. Hunt was cheerful, warm-hearted and hospitable; at his cottage in Hampstead he kept virtually open house and here Keats felt the excitement of belonging to a sympathetic intellectual community. His poem, 'Sleep and Poetry', was largely written at Hunt's cottage and its air of enthusiasm shows the beneficial effects of like-minded company and encouragement.

Hunt and his friends were liberal in their politics but the *Examiner* was markedly too radical to meet with approval in government circles. Before Keats met him Hunt had served a two-year prison sentence for libel, having published in the *Examiner* an attack on the sexual immorality of the Prince Regent (later George IV). The early nineteenth century saw an enormous increase in the number of political and literary journals, brought out to serve the interests of the rapidly expanding middle class, and the liberal *Examiner* found itself, with William Cobbett's (1762–1835) *Political Register*, frequently embattled against the more conservative *Blackwood's Edinburgh Magazine* and *The Quarterly Review*. *Blackwood's* directed jibes at

Leigh Hunt and his London-based group of writers, including Keats, under the title 'The Cockney School of Poetry'. The criticisms were overtly artistic, but the motivation behind them was political. Keats himself was never actively involved in party politics, though he was a shrewd observer, but his sympathies were undoubtedly liberal; he was amazed and amused to discover that Wordsworth, one-time supporter of the French Revolution, was campaigning in the summer of 1818 for the local Tory candidate.

Hunt's own poetry was both sentimental and jokey, his style a mixture of colloquialisms and lush extravagance. 'Swooning', 'languour', 'luxury' and 'delicious dizziness' are all characteristic of Hunt's overripe vocabulary. His influence has been widely blamed for the excesses of Keats's early style, especially in 'Endymion'. But Keats disowned Hunt's influence, claiming that any mistakes were all his own. Nevertheless Keats soon began to part company with Hunt on matters of taste, finding his egocentricity, triviality and affectation pernicious, in life and in art. (An example of Hunt's taste for whimsy is that his chosen nickname for Keats was 'Junkets'.) They never quarrelled openly, however, and Hunt remained a loyal friend; in the summer of 1820 when Keats was seriously ill and living alone in lodgings, Hunt invited him to stay for several weeks in his own crowded and chaotic household. 'Hunt has behaved very kindly to me', Keats wrote to Charles Brown shortly before he embarked for Italy.

Although Keats avoided an open quarrel with Hunt, others in his circle did not. Early in 1817 Keats found 'every Body . . . at Loggerheads'; Hunt had criticised one of Haydon's huge and ambitious paintings, the two had fallen out, and having 'known each other many years —they now live *pour ainsi dire* [French: so to speak] jealous neighbours'. Of course quarrels among friends are commonplace, but among these men feelings ran unusually high. If there is one quality the writers we now call Romantic have in common, it is their belief in the value of *feeling*. In their very different ways they shared a faith in the worth of an individual person's emotions, the value of his or her reactions to experience and the right to express or communicate these feelings. William Blake (1757–1827), sometimes called the precursor of the English Romantics, and the most startlingly individual and extreme of them all, believed so strongly in the primacy of feelings that he could write in *The Marriage of Heaven and Hell* (1790), 'Sooner murder an infant in its cradle than nurse unacted desires'. Taken literally and acted upon, such advice would have appalling consequences in terms of violence and suffering; it is not to be wondered at that more conservative sectors of society feared the anarchic consequences of unrestrained expressions of feeling. Keats never encountered Blake, who lived in relative obscurity in London, and it appears that Keats never even came across his poetry. But Keats, too, was capable in the spontaneous flow of his letters of some comparably extreme expressions of feeling: 'Nothing ever becomes real till it is experienced', 'I find that I cannot exist without poetry.'

Romanticism is sometimes described as a revolt against reason, especially the scientific rationalism of the eighteenth century, often called 'The Age of Reason', whose literature tended to be an expression of what was socially valuable rather than what was personally felt. But it is a mistake to be simplistic about this; revolutions in taste and habits of feeling tend not to happen all of a sudden and there were signs quite early in the eighteenth century in literature and in painting that feelings might be expressed rather than kept under firm control. *The Man of Feeling*, a novel by Henry Mackenzie (1745–1831), was published as early as 1771; its hero, a man of unusually tender emotions, wept and fainted in a way we would now find quite absurd. The vogue for the so-called 'Gothic Novel' is a further demonstration of the public's taste for tales of mystery, suspense and violent emotion, often set in isolated castles and abbeys (hence, 'Gothic'). *The Castle of Otranto* (1765) by Horace Walpole (1717–97) and *The Mysteries of Udolpho* (1794) by Mrs Ann Radcliffe (1764–1823) were both extremely popular novels; Keats certainly knew the latter, and so did Jane Austen (1775–1817), who satirised the genre in her own novel *Northanger Abbey* (an early work, but published posthumously in 1818). She also dramatised the conflict between reason and feeling in the novel, *Sense and Sensibility* (1811), and demonstrated through the experiences of a young girl, Marianne, that unrestrained indulgence in feeling can be destructive of oneself as well as hurtful to others. She also showed through Marianne's sister, Elinor, that a life that denies all self-expression can damage and distort the personality; clearly the ideal balance between private feeling and social relations was hard to achieve. Public opinion certainly condemned Byron and Shelley for their over-indulgence in their feelings; their unconventional relationships with women forced them into involuntary exile in Europe. But the poets hoped and believed that the expression of individual feelings would lead, not to isolation and separation, but to greater mutual understanding and social good. For Wordsworth, it should be remembered, 'Poetry is the spontaneous overflow of powerful feelings: it takes its origin from emotion recollected in tranquillity.'

'I am certain of nothing but of the holiness of the Heart's affections and the truth of Imagination', Keats wrote to Benjamin Bailey in November 1817, shortly after he had returned to London from Oxford. *Imagination* was, like feeling, a crucial concept for Keats and for many contemporary poets. Coleridge, in his work of literary biography and critical theory, *Biographia Literaria* (1817), took pains to distinguish between and, in effect, to justify different kinds and levels of imagination. He was making a case against the eighteenth-century philosophers who regarded the human mind as a mere mechanical recording device; he argued that in its ability to create something new and unique out of the raw material of its sense-impressions, the mind had a capacity almost God-like. Wordsworth, too, discussed the poetic imagination at length in his revised Preface to the *Lyrical Ballads*, published in 1815.

Keats did not, it seems, read *Biographia Literaria*, a complex work drawing heavily on eighteenth-century German philosophy. He derived many of his ideas from the critic, essayist and lecturer, William Hazlitt (1778–1830), who as a young man had been on friendly terms with Wordsworth and Coleridge. In 1818 Hazlitt gave a series of public lectures, 'On the English Poets', at the Surrey Institution in South London, in the first of which, 'On Poetry in General', he stated emphatically that 'Poetry is the language of the imagination and the passions.' For Hazlitt poetry was not a mere mirror-image of everyday reality, but a light, both direct and reflected 'that while it shows us the object, throws a sparkling radiance on all around it'. In other words, the poet's imagination does not only reflect reality, but it illuminates it; through his vision the poet throws new light on the world. For Hazlitt, 'the province of the imagination is principally visionary' and the visionary imagination is stimulated by the 'undefined' and 'uncommon'. Keats heard almost all of Hazlitt's lectures and the two men later became close friends. Hazlitt's influence on Keats's thinking on imagination, on the value of *gusto* and *intensity* in art, and on the quality of *disinterestedness* (that is, a lack of purely selfish personal concern) shows throughout the many pages of Keats's letters. The two men shared a passionate admiration for the disinterested genius of Shakespeare, and there is much of Hazlitt behind Keats's notion of Shakespeare's 'negative capability' (see p.77).

Keats did not need Hazlitt, however, to convince him of the virtues of the poetic imagination. Nor did Hazlitt introduce Keats to the idea of poet as visionary. Through his reading of Spenser, Shakespeare, Homer and, later, Milton, Keats had discovered the visionary poet's ability to create complete imaginary worlds, sometimes based on ancient myth and legend; although these visions were not in any everyday sense real they could none the less offer valuable insights into the human condition, truths to reassure and comfort men and women struggling with day-to-day problems and difficulties. Keats and Hazlitt would have argued that there is nothing merely escapist about true visionary poetry, even if it draws, as Keats's poetry often does, on as remote a subject as the mythology of ancient Greece. There is always a difficulty for both poet and reader, however, of discriminating between true vision and mere fantasy or daydream. Poets themselves were often in disagreement about the distinction. Wordsworth, for example, whose visionary experience grew from his perception of the natural landscape (particularly the mountains and lakes of Cumberland), disapproved of Keats's retreat into the Classical landscape of Arcadia. When Keats recited to him the 'Hymn to Pan' from Book I of 'Endymion', Wordsworth dismissed it as 'a Very pretty piece of Paganism'.

One of the reasons that make it so hard to define or even to describe the phenomenon, 'Romanticism', is the emphasis that it places on the *individual*. Therefore, we should not be surprised to discover how little Wordsworth, Coleridge, Keats, Shelley and Byron seem to have in common, rather than how much. While the first four of these could be described as visionaries, Byron certainly could not: his treatment, often humorous and satirical, of man in society is strongly reminiscent of the Augustan poets of the late seventeenth and early eighteenth centuries, John Dryden (1631–1700) and Alexander Pope (1688–1744). Each of the Romantics was struggling to discover and express his own vision in his individual voice; hence the diversity of subject-matter and style, the revival of long-neglected forms and the invention of new ones. It may seem strange to us now that Keats and his contemporaries devoted so much time, thought and energy to the justification of ideas that we now take so much for granted: namely, the value of individuality, imagination and originality. We use 'imaginative' quite automatically as a term of approval and we are urged at school and at work to 'use our imaginations'. That this is so is evidence of the lasting effect of the writers, artists and musicians we call the Romantics on Western culture and sensibility.

A note on the text

During Keats's lifetime forty-five of his poems were published in book form, in the three volumes, *Poems* (1817), *Endymion* (1818) and *Poems* (1820). The last was originally entitled *Lamia, Isabella, The Eve of St Agnes and Other Poems* and its contents were 'Lamia', 'Isabella', 'The Eve of St Agnes', 'Ode to a Nightingale', 'Ode on a Grecian Urn', 'Ode to Psyche', 'Fancy', 'Bards of passion and of mirth', 'Lines on the Mermaid Tavern', 'Robin Hood', 'To Autumn', 'Ode on Melancholy' and 'Hyperion'.

In addition, nine other poems were published in journals and periodicals, such as the *Annals of the Fine Arts*. After Keats's death almost a hundred other pieces were discovered and published in the later nineteenth and early twentieth centuries.

The most authoritative collection of Keats's poetry is *The Poems of*

John Keats edited by Jack Stillinger, Heinemann, London, 1978, and this is the edition quoted in these Notes. All the poems may also be found in *John Keats—The Complete Poems*, edited by John Barnard, Penguin Books, Harmondsworth, second edition, 1977.

The first selection of Keats's letters to be published was included by Richard Monckton Milnes in his *Life, Letters, and Literary Remains, of John Keats*, 1848, and later the appearance of the Keats—Fanny Brawne letters created something of a scandal in 1878. The standard modern edition is *The Letters of John Keats*, edited by Hyder Edward Rollins, Harvard University Press, Cambridge, Mass., 1958. The text quoted in these Notes is the *Letters of John Keats*, a selection edited by Robert Gittings, Oxford University Press, Oxford, 1970.

Part 2

Summaries
of SELECTED POEMS

A NOTE ON THE SONNET

Keats wrote nearly sixty sonnets and many of his earliest poems were in this form, so a brief note at this stage may be helpful.

A sonnet is a short, lyric poem of fourteen lines in one verse, or stanza. The lines are a uniform length of ten syllables in the rhythmic pattern known as iambic pentameter. That is, each line normally consists of a pattern of five units or 'feet', each of two syllables; the first syllable is lightly stressed or accented, the second syllable more strongly stressed. The stresses, or accents, are usually determined by the natural way of pronouncing the words in context. For example, we can 'scan', or mark the rhythmical pattern of the first line of one of Keats's sonnets as follows:

Frĕsh mórn/ĭng gús ts/hăve blówn/ăwáy/ăll féar

Of course, not all the stressed syllables carry exactly the same emphasis, and one might argue that 'Fresh' is just as important as the first syllable of 'morning', and that 'all' could be more strongly stressed than 'fear'. Absolute regularity is rare, and having a strong emphasis on the first syllable in a line is a common variation, as

Múch hăve/Ĭ tráv/elled ín/thĕ réalms/of góld

The sonnet form was first introduced into England in the sixteenth century. It originated in Italy and one variation of the form is called after the Italian poet, Petrarch (1304–74). The Petrarchan sonnet is recognisable by the rhyme-scheme *a b b a a b b a* in the octave, or first eight lines, and *c d c c d c* (or *c d e c d e*) in the sestet, or last six lines. Milton and Wordsworth both wrote sonnets in the Petrarchan form.

A simpler form, allowing greater freedom of choice in the rhyme-scheme, was evolved by the English sonneteers, and this became known as the Shakespearean sonnet, rhyming *a b a b c d c d e f e f g g*. The shape of the subject-matter of a sonnet is greatly affected by the pattern of the rhyme scheme: it has been said that the Petrarchan form lends itself to a statement or question followed by a resolution, whereas the Shakespearean form can repeat a problem or idea with variations in the first twelve lines, and then conclude with a neat or unexpected twist in the final couplet.

Keats wrote twice as many sonnets in the demanding Petrarchan form as he did in the Shakespearean style, making the change early in 1818 after some intensive re-reading of Shakespeare. It was from the sonnet that he gradually evolved the stanza form that he used for the great odes written in the spring of 1819.

Detailed summaries

'O, Solitude, if I must with thee dwell'

(Written in October or November, 1815; published in the *Examiner* in May 1816 and in *Poems*, 1817.)

This sonnet, the first of Keats's poems to be published though by no means the first that he composed, was written while Keats was a medical student and living in a crowded and poverty-stricken district near Guy's Hospital. Like many of his later poems it expresses his unhappiness with his present circumstances and his longing to escape to a world of natural beauty and happiness. He personifies his lonely mood as the powerful, godlike figure of solitude whose company he cannot avoid. He begs to be allowed to endure his isolation away from the city's squalor, among mountains or in deep woodlands. Then it occurs to him that his pleasure would be made almost perfect if he were allowed the company of one sympathetic friend.

The poet's image of himself in this sonnet is not unlike that of the later 'Ode on Melancholy': he dramatises himself as a humble creature in enforced service to a superior power. 'Pavillion'd', a favourite word in Keats's early verse, suggests the vault-like or canopied effect of the tracery of branches, but it also evokes the medieval chivalric romance in which heroic exploits were prefaced by nights of prayer and fasting. The rather formal air of the sonnet is reinforced by the archaic forms, 'thee' and 'thy', and there is little immediacy in the imagery of the natural landscape. The 'jumbled heap/Of murky buildings' registers as the most powerfully felt detail in the poem.

NOTES AND GLOSSARY:

steep: mountainside

Nature's observatory: natural vantage-point from which to view the stars and the distant landscape

span: handspan, the distance between thumb and little finger tips

vigils: night-long sessions of prayer and fasting

two kindred spirits: the poet's companion could have been his friend, George Felton Mathew, one of Keats's brothers or a purely imaginary being

'On First Looking into Chapman's Homer'

(Written in October 1816; published in the *Examiner*, December 1816 and reprinted in *Poems*, 1817.)

This sonnet was written in the early hours of the morning following an evening spent with Charles Cowden Clarke. Together he and Keats had read passages from the *Iliad* and the *Odyssey*, verse epics by the Greek poet, Homer (ninth or tenth century BC), translated by the poet and dramatist, George Chapman (1559–1634). Keats, who had previously read Homer only in the translations by Alexander Pope (1688–1744), was deeply impressed by the clarity and vigour of Chapman's verse, occasionally even shouting aloud in his excitement. Clarke recalled that Keats was particularly delighted by the following passage from Book V of the *Odyssey* which describes the shipwrecked Odysseus, leader of the Greek heroes returning from the Trojan Wars:

Then forth he came, his both knees falt'ring, both
His strong hands hanging down, and all with froth
His cheeks and nostrils flowing, voice and breath
Spent all to use, and down he sank to death.
The sea had soak'd his heart through.

Keats did not leave to walk home until dawn, and he must have begun to compose as soon as he reached his lodgings, for a copy of this sonnet was delivered to Clarke by ten o'clock that same morning.

The experience Keats describes in this sonnet is extremely personal and highly literary: his own excitement, as a practising poet, on discovering the works of one of the great Classical poets in an outstandingly successful translation by an English poet of the seventeenth century. But this sonnet has always been admired for the skill with which Keats dramatises his feelings, making an esoteric experience comprehensible to his readers, and convincing us of its value. By presenting himself as one of the great adventurer-explorers of the past Keats gives his literary explorations the dignity of an heroic quest. But he also touches the reader's own experience when he describes the explorer's awe at the sight of a hitherto unknown natural phenomenon, for most of us can remember something of our amazement at our first sight of a huge waterfall, a mountain, or a desert. The final image of the poem is particularly dramatic: the group of explorers frozen into silence and immobility at the sight of the vast Pacific Ocean. The placing of 'silent' at the beginning of the final line, after the slight pause of the line-division, gives it added emphasis.

Moreover, in this sonnet, as many of his contemporaries were quick to notice, Keats seemed to have discovered a new vocabulary, free of the elaborate and conventional 'poeticisms' of his earlier work (for example, see the 'river's crystal swell' and 'boughs pavillon'd' of 'O, Solitude . . . '). Like Chapman, he packs his meaning into a series of emphatic monosyllables, with hard consonants and long, resounding vowels, many of which are given additional emphasis by their position as rhyme-words: 'gold', 'told', 'deep brow'd', 'loud and bold', 'stout', 'wild'. Leigh Hunt admired the new, 'masculine' tone of this sonnet, and it has always been regarded as one of the finest of Keats's shorter poems.

NOTES AND GLOSSARY:

realms of gold:	suggests both the great age of Classical literature and El Dorado, the mythical territory rich in gold that attracted explorers to South America
bards:	wandering poets who told tales of heroes
in fealty to:	as a tenant owing loyalty to a feudal lord
Apollo:	Greek god of music and poetry
demesne:	land held by right
serene:	air (Latin: *serenum*, clear sky)
ken:	sight
stout:	brave
Cortez:	Hernando Cortez (1485–1547), Spanish explorer and conqueror of Mexico. Keats had made a mistake: it was Vasco Nunez de Balboa (1475–1517) who discovered the Pacific Ocean in 1513
Darien:	a mountainous isthmus in Central America

'On the Sea'

(Written in April 1817; published in the *Champion*, August 1817.)

The octave of the sonnet is devoted to a description of the sea, emphasising its vastness and its changing moods. Keats had seen the sea for the first time when he visited Margate in the summer of 1816 and he had been struck then by its huge and ever-changing expanse and 'Its voice mysterious' which prompts its hearers to 'think on what will be and what has been'. In the spring of 1817, when he was staying not far from the sea on the Isle of Wight and reading a good deal of Shakespeare, he wrote, 'the passage in Lear—"Do you not hear the sea?"— has haunted me intensely'. This part of the sonnet is rich in onomatopoeic effects; the gentle mood of the sea is emphasised by the hushed sound-quality of Keats's vocabulary, as 'eternal whisperings', 'shadowy sound' and 'gentle temper'. Notice the wave-like effect of the rhythm of the first two long sentences with their run-on lines (lines 1–4 and 5–8). The poem lulls and soothes the ear just as the sight of the sea calms the turbulent spirit.

The sestet is an exhortation to the reader or listener who is surfeited with the sights and sounds of busy, everyday life to find more sustaining nourishment in contemplation of the vastness of the sea. In this respect this sonnet resembles the later 'Ode on Melancholy', in which the beauty of the natural world is also regarded as food for the soul. 'On the Sea' is a much less personal poem than 'O, Solitude' or the sonnet on Chapman's Homer; the word 'I' does not occur in the poem, and the poet does not interpose his own feelings between the reader and the objects he describes. As in the ode, 'To Autumn', the poet presents an image of the world and some of its legendary associations and leaves the reader to make of it what he pleases.

NOTES AND GLOSSARY:

Hecate: Greek goddess of the moon, the night and the underworld (also known as Diana or Phoebe); as the moon-goddess she controls the tides

shadowy sound: an example of synaesthesia; that is, a sense-experience described by a term usually associated with a different sense. 'Shadowy', usually associated with sight, here describes the sound of the waves, and suggests both faintness and indistinctness as well as the darkness of the caves from which the sound comes

winds of heaven . . . unbound: in Classical mythology the god, Aeolus, gave Odysseus all the rough winds tied up in a bag so that he might have a safe voyage; unfortunately his sailors released them

quired: sang in chorus

'On Sitting Down to Read King Lear Once Again'

(Written in January 1818; not published in Keats's lifetime.)

This sonnet shows Keats reviewing his development as a poet and deliberately rejecting the seductive, musical charms of Spenserian romance in favour of the sterner vision offered by Shakespearean tragedy. He was preparing his own 'Poetic Romance', 'Endymion', for the printers at this time, and this may have prompted a reconsideration of his aims and ambitions. In 'Sleep and Poetry', written late in 1816, he had promised himself a period of indulgence in the pleasures of 'poesy', but also that this would be followed by 'a nobler life,/Where I may find the agonies, the strife/Of human hearts'. Now he feels that Romance, personified as a valiant Spenserian heroine, is a 'syren', bewitching the unwary listener with her beautiful voice. The experience of rereading Shakespeare's *King Lear* will be like enduring an ordeal by fire, in which he will be completely consumed. But Keats prays that he may be reborn as a true poet and not a mere dreamer. The distinction between the poet as dreamer or visionary was one of Keats's constant preoccupations: see the final stanza of 'Ode to a Nightingale' and 'The Fall of Hyperion', Book I, line 198, 'Art thou not of the dreamer tribe?'.

This is the thirty-fifth Petrarchan sonnet that Keats wrote, and it was to be almost his last in this particular form. The sestet concludes with a characteristically Shakespearean rhyming couplet, a prayer for greater poetic powers.

NOTES AND GLOSSARY:

King Lear: the tragedy by William Shakespeare, first performed in 1606, in which the old King abdicates and then suffers greatly at the hands of two of his daughters

plumed syren: in Classical legend, the sirens were three women who lured sailors to their death by the sweetness of their singing; Odysseus escaped them by having himself tied to the mast and plugging his sailors' ears with wax; Romance is pictured wearing a plumed helmet

assay: try out, test (especially the quality of metals)

Chief Poet: Shakespeare

Albion: an ancient name for Britain. The action of *King Lear* is set in Britain

Phoenix: a legendary bird, said to live for five hundred years and then to burn to death on a funeral pyre and rise again from the ashes. Sometimes a symbol of the resurrection of Christ

---

'When I have fears that I may cease to be'

(Written in January 1818; not published in Keats's lifetime.)

Written only a few days after the *King Lear* sonnet, this poem shows even more clearly the extent of Shakespeare's influence on Keats at this time. Keats has adopted the freer pattern of the Shakespearean rhyme scheme (*a b a b c d c d e f e f g g*) and the subject-matter, his fear that death will deny him fame as a poet and frustrate his desire for love, echoes Shakespeare's dread of 'Time's injurious hand'. (For example, see Shakespeare's sonnets, 'When I have seen by Time's fell hand defaced' and 'Like as the waves make towards the pebbled shore'.)

His friend, Richard Woodhouse, reported that Keats never sat down to write unless his head was crammed full of ideas, and Keats himself maintained that 'if Poetry comes not as naturally as the Leaves to a tree it had better not come at all'. The imagery of this sonnet clearly illustrates Keats's feelings about the process of composition: 'teeming' suggests the prodigious fertility of the brain which, like the soil, produces an abundant harvest to be reaped by the poet's pen and stored on the printed page. It is a process both natural, inevitable and beyond the poet's control. In spite of the resolutions of the *King Lear* sonnet Keats has still not relinquished his visions of 'high romance' as the subject-matter of his poetry, however. In the last few lines, contemplation of the wide expanse of the sea drives all mere personal concern with love and fame out of his head.

NOTES AND GLOSSARY:

glean'd: literally, picked up every ear of corn dropped by the harvesters

teeming: literally, reproducing or giving birth in huge numbers

charactery: (Shakespearean) letters, handwritten or printed

fair creature of an hour: a beautiful woman whom Keats has known only for a short time (not Fanny Brawne, whom Keats did not meet until later in 1818)

'The Eve of St Agnes'

(Written early in 1819; published in *Poems*, 1820).

Keats probably began this poem a few days before the feast-day of St Agnes which, in the Christian calendar, falls on 21 January. Writing fast, he completed the poem in about nine days between 18 January and 2 February 1819. Keats's subject is based on the ancient superstition that on the night before the festival of St Agnes a young girl might dream of her future husband or lover if she performed certain rituals before she went to bed. These rituals included prayer and fasting (that is, abstaining from food), not speaking, not looking behind her or to either side, and finally lying in bed on her back without moving. In a draft stanza which did not appear in the final version of the poem Keats described the dream which would follow this process of self-denial: first the girl's 'future lord' would offer her delicious food, sweets and wine, then she would hear music, and eventually, Keats hints, she would experience in full the delights of erotic love. In spite of the seeming reality of her dream she would wake in the morning as pure a virgin as the night before.

'The Eve of St Agnes' was Keats's third narrative poem and, like 'Endymion' (written in 1817 and published in 1818) and 'Isabella; or, The Pot of Basil' (written early in 1818 and published in *Poems*, 1820), it is a love-story. However, unlike 'Isabella', a tragic tale of unhappy love in which the heroine weeps over the flower-pot in which her dead lover's head is buried, 'The Eve of St Agnes' is a tale of love triumphant: the hero risks death to win his beloved and together they escape unharmed. Elements in Keats's poem echo Shakespeare's *Romeo and Juliet* (*c*. 1595): the feuding families, the old nurse who helps the lovers to their secret meeting, and the hero's veneration of his beloved (each lover reveres his lady's saintly virtue and addresses her as his 'shrine'). But Keats owes more to Edmund Spenser than to Shakespeare. 'The Eve of St Agnes' is his most complete recreation of medieval romance, the world of chivalry, magic and 'amour courtois' (courtly love) revived by Spenser at the end of the sixteenth century. The language of 'The Eve of St Agnes' is full of terms borrowed from Spenser, such as 'amort', 'quoth', 'affray'd'; many of the forms of verbs and pronouns are also archaic, such as 'laugheth' for 'laughs', 'pattereth' for 'patters', and 'Hie thee' for 'You should get away.' But Keats's most conspicuous borrowing is the stanza form devised by Spenser for his epic poem in the style of a medieval romance, *The Faerie Queene*.

The Spenserian stanza is a demanding verse form with a severely restricted number of rhymes: only three are allowed for the stanza's nine lines, in the pattern *a b a b b c b c c*. The first eight lines have ten syllables while the last line has twelve, and this longer final line with its clinching couplet rhyme brings each stanza to an emphatic conclusion. The rhythm is generally iambic (alternate unstressed and stressed syllables), with some variations, especially in the long final line. Although Spenser was undoubtedly his original model, early in 1819 Keats referred to a poem he enjoyed, 'The Castle of Indolence' (1748) by James Thomson (1700–48), and this, too, had been written in Spenserian stanzas.

Keats wrote 'The Eve of St Agnes' shortly after he had abandoned his projected epic poem, 'Hyperion', over which he had laboured for several months. In spite of its length (378 lines in 42 stanzas), Keats referred to 'The Eve of St Agnes' rather dismissively as 'a little poem' and it must have seemed to him a very slight affair compared with the weighty 'Hyperion'. He worried that both it and 'Isabella' were, in contemporary slang, too 'smokeable', that is, liable to satirical criticism for being too 'weak-sided' and showing 'too much inexperience of life and simplicity of knowledge'. He knew how seductively easy it was to slip into fantasy, and he was well aware of the public's continuing appetite for the marvels and horrors of 'Gothic' fictions; he referred rather drily to the 'fine mother Radcliffe names' he had chosen for his poem. But Keats was not the only poet of his generation to serve this particular taste; Coleridge's 'Christabel', an unfinished poem published in 1816, contains many Gothic elements: events take place at night in a baronial castle in an atmosphere of mysterious enchantment and brooding evil. And 'The Lay of the Last Minstrel' (1805) by Sir Walter Scott (1771–1832) is a tale of young lovers separated by a family feud who, after many trials and sufferings, achieve happiness.

It is clear from many details in 'The Eve of St Agnes' that Keats knew both these poems and borrowed freely from them.

In your reading of 'The Eve of St Agnes' notice how Keats makes the imaginary world of the poem seem real through vivid, physical details. Precise details of dress, weapons, architecture and the language of heraldry help to give the impression of an authentic historical background. And, in addition, notice how Keats's frequent appeals to the five senses contribute to the changing atmosphere and mood of the poem; the story builds towards its climax through a series of contrasts between extremes of sensation, so that when the crucial moment comes the reader's own senses are in a state of heightened, sympathetic awareness. The opening stanzas of the poem offer a violent contrast between opposed extremes: darkness, silence and bitter cold give way to bright light, trumpet music and warmth. As the poem develops Keats plays continually on the contrasts between age and youth, brutality and tenderness, uproar and silence, sensual and spiritual.

'The Eve of St Agnes' has often been described as a triumph of descriptive and lyrical skill, but for Keats this was not enough. Later in 1819 he wrote, 'I wish to diffuse the colouring of St Agnes' Eve throughout a Poem in which character and Sentiment would be the figures to such drapery.'

Stanzas 1 to 8

On St Agnes' Eve, a bitterly cold winter night, an aged pensioner returns from his prayers through an empty chapel where the cold is so intense that even the stone figures on the tombs seem to freeze. The old man hears sounds of distant music, but continues on his way to pray for his own soul and for the souls of all sinners. In the castle above music echoes through the great chambers as preparations are made for a feast. Crowds of guests arrive, magnificently robed and jewelled, but the narrator points out one lady who has thoughts only for the legend of St Agnes. This lady, Madeline, ignores her many admirers, oblivious of everything but her longed-for dream of love.

NOTES AND GLOSSARY:

St Agnes: a Christian Saint and virgin martyr, executed in Rome in the fourth century AD, always depicted with a lamb, the symbol of purity

Beadsman: a pensioner who is paid to pray for the souls of his benefactors; like all Roman Catholics he uses a rosary, or string of beads, to help in his devotions

Flatter'd to tears: the Beadsman weeps because the music offers him false promises and empty hopes of pleasure; he is too old for dancing and love

carved angels:	in the Gothic architecture of the Middle Ages the ends of the roof beams in churches were often decorated with carved figures of angels
argent:	silver, a term from the language of heraldry
Madeline:	Keats thought the name beautiful, but there may also be a connection with Mary Magdalene in the Bible, who, once a prostitute, repented of her sins with tears and became a follower of Christ
timbrels:	tambourines
amort:	dead (one of the many archaisms in the poem)

Stanzas 9 to 21

Meanwhile Porphyro approaches the castle, praying for a chance to see his beloved Madeline. Risking death at the hands of Madeline's barbarous kinsmen, he enters the castle. Only one old woman, Madeline's nurse Angela, takes pity on him and she urges him to escape before he is discovered and killed. Porphyro begs Angela to take him to Madeline and then, when he hears of her belief in the St Agnes myth, he persuades Angela to help him to hide in Madeline's bedchamber. Reluctantly the old woman agrees and hurries off to bring a selection of delicacies from the feast.

NOTES AND GLOSSARY:

Porphyro:	from the Greek for 'purple'; porphyry is a hard, purple or red rock (and red is traditionally the colour of passion); Porphyrius (AD 233−c. 306) was a Neoplatonist philosopher and enemy of Christianity
holy loom:	on the feast of St Agnes in Rome the wool of two consecrated lambs was woven into a robe for a priest
mickle:	much (dialect, Scottish or Northern English)
purple riot:	Keats is punning on Porphyro's name: excitement is making his heart beat faster, pumping the red (purple) blood violently
betide her weal or woe:	whatever good or evil happens to her (archaic)
Merlin paid his Demon:	a puzzling reference to Merlin, the benign magician of Arthurian legend, who confessed his secrets to the beautiful Nimue; she later destroyed him. This allusion casts a sinister light on the night's events and suggests that playing with magic may be dangerous
cates and dainties:	delicious foods (archaic)
tambour frame:	circular frame on which fabric is stretched for embroidery

took covert:	found a hiding-place; 'covert' is used in hunting for the shelter of the fox, deer or other game
amain:	greatly (archaic)

Stanzas 22 to 32

Madeline enters her bedchamber as Porphyro watches from his hiding-place. As she kneels in prayer the moonlight streaming through a stained-glass window bathes her in colour and forms a halo round her head; she seems a divine creature and Porphyro almost faints as he watches her. Then she removes her jewellery, slowly and dreamily takes off her clothes, gets into bed and, still thinking of St Agnes, gently drifts off to sleep. When Porphyro is sure that she is sleeping soundly he emerges from his hiding-place and silently arranges a collection of delicious fruits and exotic delicacies on a table. He tries to awaken Madeline, but she is spellbound in sleep and for a while Porphyro waits beside her, lost in daydreams himself.

NOTES AND GLOSSARY:

fray'd:	frightened (archaic)
balmy:	fragrant, soothing; from 'balm', sweet-smelling ointment made from the resin of trees and the sap of plants
casement:	the description of the stained-glass window with its elaborate stone tracery is one of the most vivid visual images in the poem; the diamond-shaped glass panes contain heraldic emblems, shield-shaped coats-of-arms denoting royal marriages, and images of saints. Many of the details may have been drawn from a Gothic chapel at Stansted, near Chichester, which Keats visited in January 1819
emblazonings:	heraldic term for the device painted on a shield to identify its owner
scutcheon:	coat-of-arms
blush'd with blood:	literally, was coloured red; metaphorically this suggests both the blood shed in battle and the blood of royal lineage
gules:	the heraldic term for red. Keats here makes the same mistake as Sir Walter Scott (1771–1832) in his poetic romance, 'The Lay of the Last Minstrel' (1805): moonlight does not in fact transmit the colours of stained glass. See Scott's poem, Canto II, stanza 11, 'The moon-beam kiss'd the holy pane,/And threw on the pavement a bloody stain . . . ' This inaccuracy, or poetic licence, does not detract from the power of Keats's imagery

glory: halo or aureole, traditionally pictured round the head of a saint in Christian art

poppied warmth of sleep: the poppy is associated with sleep since one variety produces the narcotic drug, opium

Clasp'd like a missal . . . pray: meaning unclear, but possibly 'Held as firmly as a Christian would grasp his prayer-book in a non-Christian (Muslim) country'

Morphean amulet: Morpheus is the god of sleep; 'amulet' is a charm to ward off evil. Porphyro wants a magic spell to keep Madeline asleep until his preparations are complete

clarion: sound of a trumpet

soother: a word invented by Keats: both 'smoother' and 'more soothing'

Manna: in the Bible, the food provided by God for the Israelites in the wilderness; here, probably a sweet fruit

eremite: religious recluse or hermit (See also the sonnet, 'Bright Star', line 4)

woofed: woven; the threads running at right-angles on a loom are called the warp (running lengthwise) and the woof

Stanzas 33 to 42
Porphyro plays a love-song on Madeline's lute; she wakes and is distressed to find the real Porphyro so much more pale and sad than the figure she has just dreamed of. She weeps, fearing that he may die and leave her alone. Her distress intensifies Porphyro's desire and he makes love to her; Madeline's dream is now reality. She still fears that Porphyro will desert her, but he swears that he will love and worship her for ever and persuades her to escape with him under cover of the storm that is now raging outside. Together they hurry along the dark, windy passages, past the sleeping guards and out through the heavy castle door. This all happened, the narrator reminds us, long ago; and on the night that the lovers escaped Madeline's kinsmen suffered terrible nightmares, old Angela died paralysed and deformed, and the aged pensioner, having said his prayers, slept forgotten among his penitential ashes.

NOTES AND GLOSSARY:

'La belle dame sans mercy': the title of a French poem, 'The beautiful lady without pity' by the fifteenth-century poet, Alain Chartier. (See also Keats's poem of the same name)

Stanzas 35 and 36: Keats certainly intended his readers to believe that Porphyro made love to Madeline while she was in a state between dream and full wakefulness. In the autumn of 1819 Keats revised the text of stanza 35 so that the last two lines ran: 'See, while she speaks his arms encroaching slow,/Have zoned her, heart to heart,—loud, loud the dark winds blow!' And in stanza 36 the fifth and sixth lines ran 'With her wild dream he mingled, as a rose/Marrieth its odour to a violet.' But the publishers found these changes too sexually explicit and 'unfit for ladies', so the version printed in *Poems*, 1820, was the one which now appears in all modern editions

Solution sweet: an oblique reference to the lovers' sexual union

flaw-blown: blown by a gust of wind

vassal: slave (archaic)

vermeil: scarlet (a term used by Spenser)

haggard: wild, fierce

wassaillers: revellers who have been drinking wine and ale

Rhenish: German wine from the Rhine region

dragons: not the mythical monsters, but 'dragoons', soldiers who in battle were mounted on horseback and armed with guns

arras: an embroidered wall-hanging, tapestry

thousand aves: many repetitions of the prayer which begins, 'Ave Maria' (Latin for 'Hail Mary'); the Beadsman will have 'told' or counted his prayers with his string of rosary beads

Although the story of 'The Eve of St Agnes' is both slight and fantastic it is one of Keats's most dramatic poems and also one which conveys a strong sense of actuality. It is dramatic in its succession of scenes, in each of which time, place and atmosphere are rapidly and vividly suggested. It is, perhaps, less dramatic in the realisation of fully defined characters, although the dialogue exchanges between Porphyro and Angela are vigorous and individual. But the poem is most dramatic in the immediacy of Keats's presentation of thoughts, actions and feelings. In other words, at crucial points in the action the reader has the impression of events actually taking place *now*, as he or she reads. For example, from stanza 23 to stanza 27 the narrator describes events from Porphyro's point of view as, from his hiding-place, he watches Madeline undress. And in stanza 26 Keats emphasises the mood of rising sexual excitement by shifting from the narrative past to the more dramatic present tense: 'his heart *revives* ... her hair she *frees* ...

Unclasps her warmed jewels . . . *Loosens* her fragrant boddice . . . ' The same shift occurs in stanza 36: 'Intó her dream he *melted* . . . meantime the frost-wind *blows* . . . ', jolting the lovers and the reader from bliss to the harsh conditions of present reality. As the lovers make their escape in stanza 41, once again the tense slips into the present, reinforcing their haste and urgency: 'they *glide* . . . the bolts full easy *slide* . . . The key *turns*, and the door upon its hinges *groans*'.

The poem has often been admired, especially by the Pre-Raphaelite poets of the later nineteenth century, for its brilliant pictorial quality. Keats's visual imagery is noticeably powerful, especially his emotive and even symbolic use of colour. In the early part of the poem there is little direct reference to colour; significantly, the first term is 'black' (stanza 2), followed by 'golden' (stanza 3), 'silver' (stanza 4), 'argent' (stanza 5) and 'lily white' (stanza 6). Into this almost monochrome world the glowing colours of stanzas 24 and 25 burst like a life-giving fountain, and although Madeline is illuminated like a saint, the flush of red on her breast and the 'Rose-bloom' on her hands remind us that she is also a desirable, sexual creature, for in Western culture red is associated with passion and the rose is the symbol of carnal as well as of spiritual love.

Keats's suggestive use of colour-symbolism and his many references to Christianity and paganism have prompted some commentators to search for an allegorical interpretation of the poem. But it is difficult to see 'The Eve of St Agnes' as a battle between the spiritual and the sensual in which one or other triumphs. 'The Eve of St Agnes' is powerfully, if indirectly, erotic; consider the intimate suggestion of body heat and the contact with skin in Madeline's 'warmed jewels', and the mouth-watering anticipation of succulent delights in stanza 30. Madeline may be associated with the lily and the dove, Christian symbols of chastity, innocence and gentleness, but it is she who wishes to dream of her lover and is prepared to dabble in magic in order to do so. Porphyro, on the other hand, although he may seem little more than the personification of youthful lust (and he indulges in some rather questionable Peeping Tom-ism in Madeline's bedroom), claims to worship Madeline as a saint and sees himself as a 'famish'd pilgrim, —saved by miracle'. For him, love is a holy as well as a passionate relationship. If 'The Eve of St Agnes' is a celebration of a love that unites the sacred and the sensual, it is also a reminder that such youthful bliss is only a small part of experience. The opening and closing stanzas of the poem prohibit sentimentality by their forceful demonstration that 'In the midst of life we are in death'. This idea would have been familiar to Keats from his knowledge of the art and literature of the Renaissance, where the grotesque figure of Death with his scythe often accompanies young lovers in their garden of delights, as well as from his own recent experience of the death of his brother, Tom.

'Bright star, would I were stedfast as thou art'

(Written in 1819, possibly in the spring; not published in Keats's lifetime.)

This sonnet, Shakespearean in form, is traditionally associated with Fanny Brawne, who is assumed to be the 'fair love' of line 10. She herself copied the sonnet into a translation of the *Inferno* by Dante (1265–1321) which Keats had given her. In April 1819 Keats described a dream he had had after reading Dante's account in Canto V of the *Inferno* of his meeting with the lovers, Paolo and Francesca:

> The dream was one of the most delightful enjoyments I ever had in my life—I floated about the whirling atmosphere . . . with a beautiful figure to whose lips mine were joined as it seem'd for an age— and in the midst of all this cold and darkness I was warm—

There is a striking similarity between the dream and this sonnet, particularly in the contrast between the cold, dark space and the warmth of the lovers' embrace. At about this time Keats had discussed with Coleridge 'Different genera and species of Dreams . . . a dream accompanied by a sense of touch—single and double touch—a dream related.' Keats's own dream could have featured in this conversation, especially since, in an earlier and more openly erotic draft of the sonnet, lines 10 and 11 ran 'Cheek-pillowed on my Love's white ripening breast/To touch for ever its warm sink and swell . . .'

Like the Spring odes, this sonnet expresses a longing for permanence; 'stedfast' means 'firmly in position', 'unchanging', but it also carries the moral connotation of faithfulness and endurance. In the first eight lines of the poem Keats simultaneously elaborates and rejects an image of steadfastness; he builds a picture of dark, cold and emptiness watched over by the hermit-like star and ritually cleansed by the purifying tides. This ascetic image is then rejected in favour of the tender eroticism of the last five lines; Keats longs to be held eternally in the 'sweet unrest' that precedes love-making. The moment to be preserved is the exquisite peak of anticipation, like the lovers on the Grecian Urn, 'For ever warm and still to be enjoyed'. Notice how, like 'The Eve of St Agnes', this sonnet works through a series of contrasts: Keats sets the intimacy of the warm, gently-breathing bodies of the final lines against the background of vast, cold, dark spaces, the lonely, hermit-like star and the chaste purity of sea and snow-covered hills.

NOTES AND GLOSSARY:

Eremite: a religious recluse (see 'The Eve of St Agnes', line 277)

ablution: washing, with the sense of ritual purification

swoon to death: Keats had previously associated 'swoon' with sexual ecstasy (see 'Endymion', Book I, line 398). There may be a play on words here: in Elizabethan poetry the act of love was often referred to as 'the little death'

'La Belle Dame sans Merci: A Ballad'

(Written in April 1819; published in the *Indicator*, May 1820).

Traditionally, a ballad is a poem that tells a story of exciting, heroic or even supernatural events. Originally, ballads were sung or recited to an audience and the story moved rapidly through action and dialogue. Many of the most popular ballads were handed down by word of mouth through the centuries and exist in several different versions, altered and improved by generations of minstrels (that is, musicians and entertainers) and local storytellers. The Romantic poets were interested in the ballad as an authentic, native poetic form; Sir Walter Scott published his three-volume collection of traditional ballads, *Minstrelsy of the Scottish Border*, in 1802–3, and Wordsworth and Coleridge adopted the ballad form in their first joint collection of poems, *Lyrical Ballads* (1798). Short as it is, 'La Belle Dame' resembles in many ways Coleridge's much longer ballad, 'The Rime of the Ancient Mariner' (published in *Lyrical Ballads*); each presents an encounter between a mortal and a supernatural being and the blighted life that follows this encounter, and both poems have an eerie, nightmarish atmosphere.

In this poem Keats uses a variation of the most common ballad stanza form, which is a four-line stanza (quatrain), rhyming *a b c b*. Normally the lines have about eight syllables (ballads are seldom absolutely regular), with four stresses in the first and third lines, and three stresses in the second and fourth lines. Keats makes the fourth line shorter: it has only two stresses and, usually, only four syllables. This gives each stanza a curiously unfinished feeling, a sense of having been abruptly broken off. (Read the poem aloud and see whether you agree, and whether you think this effect complements the experience the poem describes.) The frequent repetition of words, phrases and even whole lines is another typical feature of the ballad; this would have aided the memories of both reciters and listeners as well as emphasising points in the story when long ballads were spoken aloud. In spite of its apparent simplicity, 'La Belle Dame' is a powerful, haunting poem and the many repetitions contribute to its strangely hypnotic effect.

In the first three stanzas the narrator questions a solitary knight and asks him why he wanders alone in the bleak, wintry countryside, and why he looks so mortally ill. The rest of the poem consists of the knight's reply. He explains that he once met a beautiful lady out in the countryside and fell in love with this strange, fairylike creature who seemed also to have fallen in love with him. But when he had taken her to her cavern home, she broke down and wept wildly and he had to soothe her to sleep with kisses. Then he himself had a terrible dream in which ghostly figures warned him that he had been taken prisoner by 'La Belle Dame sans Merci', and on waking he found himself on the bare hillside where he has been wandering ever since.

NOTES AND GLOSSARY:

La Belle Dame sans Merci: *(French)* The Beautiful Lady without Pity, the title of a poem by the fifteenth-century French poet, Alain Chartier. (See also stanza 33 of 'The Eve of St Agnes')

knight-at-arms: a soldier, usually of noble birth, who in the Middle Ages fought on horseback wearing armour and carrying a spear, sword and shield

lily, rose: metaphor describing the white and red of an ideally beautiful complexion; the lily is also associated with purity and chastity, and the rose with amorous passion

fragrant zone: scented girdle (made of flowers); in legend the 'zone' or magical girdle of Venus, goddess of love and beauty, gave beauty and grace to the wearer and inspired love

made sweet moan: an expression common in medieval romances meaning sang, or murmured, sweetly

manna: sweet-tasting food; in the Bible it was miraculously supplied to feed the Israelites in the wilderness (see Exodus, 16). This line recalls Coleridge's 'Kubla Khan': 'For he on honey-dew hath fed/And drunk the milk of Paradise'

grot: cave, fantastically shaped

in thrall: enslaved

gloam: from 'gloaming', twilight, dusk

First and subsequent readings of this poem leave the reader puzzling over a number of questions, such as 'Is the lady deliberately evil?', 'How can the knight be sure she loves him if she speaks a strange language?', 'Why does she weep and sigh?', 'Why does the knight linger on the bare hillside? Or is he spellbound and unable to escape?' and 'Has his experience been real or mere illusion?'. The language of the poem is direct and simple, in true ballad style, but even after many close readings these questions remain unanswered; the poem is enigmatic, tantalisingly inexplicit, and consequently has attracted a wide variety of interpretations. For some the lady represents Love, Death by

Consumption, or Poetry, while others see in her a reference to Fanny Brawne (but it should be remembered that Keats had written poetry about the quest for love long before he had met her). He was certainly familiar with many of the myths of enchantresses who beguiled men with their beauty and then held them captive by witchcraft, such as the sorceress, Circe, who turned Odysseus's sailors into pigs, and Keats could have read many such legends in Chapman's translation of Homer and a recently published translation of Dante's *Inferno*. There is no doubt that he also had the deceiving enchantresses of *The Faerie Queene* in mind, for he had referred to Spenser's 'false Florimel' (an evil spirit masquerading as a figure of chastity and virtue) in the letter which contains the earliest known manuscript version of 'La Belle Dame sans Merci'. Keats's debt to Spenser shows also in the many archaisms, such as 'made sweet moan' and 'sigh'd full sore'.

Recognition of the many literary echoes in the poem is not indispensable to an appreciation of its peculiar, haunting quality. Notice, particularly, the effect of the repetition of sounds, words, phrases and even whole stanzas. The last stanza does not exactly echo the first, however: 'The sedge *has* wither'd...' becomes 'Though the sedge *is* wither'd...' implying that, for the knight, time has stopped and he lives in a perpetual winter. Listen to the melancholy effect of the repeated long 'o' sounds: 'O...alone...no...woe-begone...rose ...zone...moan...cold...gloam...awoke...cold...no...' And notice how the characteristic ballad-style alliteration reinforces the hypnotic quality of the poem: 'Her hair was *l*ong, her foot was *l*ight', '*m*ade sweet *m*oan', '*w*ild *w*ild *ey*es'. In his letter to his brother and sister-in-law Keats referred to the poem facetiously; he explained that there had to be *four* kisses in stanza 8 because 'I was obliged to choose an even number that both eyes might have fair play.' Nevertheless, 'La Belle Dame sans Merci' deals sombrely with the pain of lost love and vanished happiness, one of Keats's major themes. In a later narrative poem, 'Lamia', Keats developed more fully the story of a fatal love between a mortal and an immortal and there, too, the central character is ambiguous and judgement on her remains suspended.

THE ODES OF 1819

In the long letter to his brother and sister-in-law which contained 'La Belle Dame sans Merci', Keats also included a sonnet, 'If by dull rhymes our English must be chain'd', which expressed his impatience with the restrictions of the sonnet form and his determination to construct 'Sandals more interwoven and complete/To fit the naked foot of Poesy'. His subsequent experiments with the longer, less regular form of the ode resulted in his finest group of poems, the odes written in the spring of 1819 and, a few months later, the ode 'To Autumn'.

Keats was by no means the first or only one of his contemporaries to write odes. Wordsworth's 'Ode to Duty' and 'Ode on Intimations of Immortality' were published in 1807, and Coleridge's 'Dejection' ode had been printed in a newspaper in 1802 before it appeared in his collection, *Sybilline Leaves*, in 1817. But the ode did not originate in nineteenth-century England; its roots are in Classical antiquity. At the turn of the sixth and fifth centuries BC the Greek poet, Pindar, wrote odes to celebrate the prowess of the winners at the Olympic games, poems whose long, complex stanzas (or strophes) were arranged in groups of three like the pattern of the chorus of a Greek drama (strophe, antistrophe and epode). Elements of the Classical ode survived when English poets of the seventeenth and eighteenth centuries adopted the form; John Dryden's ode, 'To the Pious Memory of Mistress Anne Killigrew' (1686) is a poem of praise addressed to an individual, but sometimes odes were addressed to an abstract idea, such as Thomas Gray's (1716–71) 'Hymn to Adversity' (1753), or even to a time of day, such as William Collins's (1721–59) 'Ode to Evening' (1746). The movement of the ode, through question and answer, or opposing statements, to a resolution also survived in poems of meditation or inner debate where ideas or moods changed from stanza to stanza and progressed towards a conclusion. Individual poets developed their own versions of the complicated, irregular stanza; Wordsworth and Coleridge alternated long and short stanzas, whereas Keats evolved a regular, ten-line verse form.

Irritated though he was by the limitations of the sonnet, Keats still clung to it closely in the design of his new ode stanza. The stanzas of the 'Ode to Psyche', generally considered the earliest of the Spring odes, appear irregular, but Keats seldom breaks out of iambic pentameter and the rhyme scheme is dominated by Shakespearean and Petrarchan sonnet patterns. The four later Spring odes combine a Shakespearean quatrain (rhyming *a b a b*) with a Petrarchan sestet (rhyming *c d e c d e*, *c d e d c e*, etc). Notice how in almost every stanza the conclusion of the quatrain marks a break in the sense or thought-process and notice, also, the shift in mood from the snappy, 'pouncing' rhymes (Keats's own word) of the quatrain to the subtler, extended pattern of the sestet. It has often been said that Keats's odes are closer in style and mood to a Shakespearean sonnet sequence than they are to the traditional English ode. Their length gives scope for the development of thought and feeling, while retaining the density and concentration of the sonnet form.

'Ode to Psyche'

(Written in April, 1819; published in *Poems*, 1820.)
According to Classical legend, Psyche was a beautiful nymph with

whom Cupid, the mischievous young love-god who had hitherto been immune to all tender emotions, fell in love. Psyche's disobedience and the jealousy of Venus (Cupid's mother and the goddess of love) caused the lovers to suffer a long separation, but after Psyche had undergone many hardships they were reunited and, at Cupid's request, Jupiter, the father of the gods, made Psyche immortal and a goddess. 'Psyche' is the Greek word for 'soul', so the love-story of Cupid and Psyche is also an allegorical account of how the human soul achieved immortality: the soul is discovered by love, suffers because of its own disobedience and is eventually reunited with love and given eternal life. 'Psyche' also means 'butterfly' so Psyche is often represented with wings, signifying the lightness of the soul as it rises from the body after death.

Keats had certainly been thinking about the value of suffering at the time that he wrote the 'Ode to Psyche', for a few pages before he copied it into his long letter to George and Georgiana Keats he had written, 'Call the world if you Please "The vale of Soul-making" . . . . Do you not see how necessary a World of Pains and troubles is to school an Intelligence and make it a Soul?' But in the ode Keats seems less concerned with the story of Psyche's love and suffering than with her status as a newly-created goddess and with himself as her worshipper. In the first strophe he claims to have seen with 'awakened', visionary eyes Psyche and her lover, Cupid, lying peacefully together in a forest glade. (Although Cupid is not named in the poem he is undoubtedly the 'winged boy' of line 21 and the 'warm Love' of line 67.) In the second and third strophes the poet regrets that Psyche, the most beautiful goddess on Olympus, has no temple or worshippers of her own; deified when worship of the Olympians had already begun to decline, she has neither priests, ceremonies nor music in her honour. At the end of the third strophe the poet offers himself as her worshipper, and in the fourth he promises to build her a temple in his own mind, and to create in his imagination a beautiful, pastoral landscape where she may safely await the arrival of her lover.

With the exception of T.S. Eliot (1888–1965), who admired it the most of all the odes, most critics have tended to treat the 'Ode to Psyche' dismissively, regarding it as an over-elaborate piece of pseudo-Classicism in the manner of 'Endymion'. But it is also possible to read the poem as Keats's re-dedication of his poetic imagination to the service of the human soul, in this instance personified as a beautiful young woman, both loving and beloved. (In 'Sleep and Poetry' (1817) Keats had looked forward to a maturer phase of his poetic development, 'a nobler life,/Where I may find the agonies, the strife/Of human hearts'.) In this ode Keats adds to the tale of Psyche, her love and her elevation to divine status, which is itself an allegory, a new and very personal allegorical dimension. Since the human soul is inadequately worshipped in the present, irreligious age, Keats will create in his imagination an ideal domain where the soul can flourish and encounter love. In this sense the ode makes bold claims for the power of the poetic imagination to create a world infinitely superior to the conditions of everyday reality, and for the humanitarian ideals of the poet.

NOTES AND GLOSSARY:

Psyche: Keats had referred to the legend of Psyche in one of his earliest poems, 'I stood tip-toe upon a little hill': legend had it that Cupid first visited Psyche incognito, at night, but she, curious to see who her lover was, lit a lamp and spilt a drop of hot oil on Cupid's shoulder. He immediately awoke and fled, and this began the long period of Psyche's penitential wanderings: 'The silver lamp,—the ravishment,—the wonder—/The darkness,—loneliness, —the fearful thunder;/Their woes gone by, and both to heaven upflown,/To bow for gratitude before Jove's throne'

numbers: verses

conched: convoluted, like a conch shell

Tyrian: ancient Tyre, on the coast of present-day Lebanon, was famous for its purple dyes

pinions: wings

eye-dawn of aurorean love: in Classical legend Aurora was the goddess of the dawn, so the phrase means, 'as their eyes open their love is renewed like the rising sun'

Olympus' faded hierarchy: the old order of Greek gods, whose home was said to be Mount Olympus, were no longer so fervently worshipped when Psyche was added to their number. The legend of Cupid was included in *The Golden Ass* by Apuleius in the second century AD and translated into English in the sixteenth century

Phoebe's ... star: the moon; in Greek myth Phoebe was the goddess of the moon

Vesper, amorous: the evening star, the planet Venus, thus associated with love

make delicious moan: sing beautiful songs (see also 'La Belle Dame sans Merci')

censer: perforated metal container in which sweet-smelling incense is burned to give pleasure to the god; the rising smoke also symbolises the prayers of the worshippers

teeming:	pouring, flowing
oracle:	voice of a god speaking through a human inter-mediary who is in a trance
heat/Of pale-mouthed prophet:	'heat' signifies divine inspiration, but in his tranced state the priest is pale as he foretells the future
antique vows:	worship offered in ancient times
fond believing lyre:	hymns sung to the harp by faithful, devoted worshippers
so far retir'd/From happy pieties:	so far removed from the habit of joyful worship
lucent fans:	shining wings
faint Olympians:	as the gods of Olympus are no longer worshipped, they are growing weak and gradually disappearing
fane:	temple, shrine
branched thoughts:	a powerful image, suggesting both the elaborate workings of the imagination and the organic struc-ture of the brain
pleasant pain:	suggests both the labour and the delight of crea-tion, but this paradox is a constant preoccupation in the odes: see 'Ode to a Nightingale' and 'Ode on Melancholy'
Fledge:	cover, literally with feathers
zephyrs:	in Classical myth, gentle West winds
Dryads:	in Classical myth, tree-nymphs
gardener Fancy:	Fancy, or imagination, as a gardener who can improve on wild nature was an idea much debated by Shakespeare and his contemporaries; Keats's own poem, 'Fancy', ends 'Let the winged Fancy roam,/Pleasure never is at home'
feign:	invent
shadowy thought:	possibly, vague and unclear ideas, or the myster-ious process of imagination
casement:	according to legend, Cupid flew in through Psyche's window at night; see also a similar image at the end of 'Ode to a Nightingale'

In his long letter to his brother and sister-in-law Keats claimed that this poem 'is the first and the only one with which I have taken even moderate pains—I have for the most part dash'd off my lines in a hurry'. Given the care with which Keats redrafted sections of 'The Eve of St Agnes', we may take this statement with a pinch of salt, but Keats continued, 'I think it reads the more richly for it and will I hope encourage me to write other things in a more peacable and healthy spirit'. Some might argue that Keats did not achieve real serenity and repose of mind until the ode 'To Autumn', but the 'Ode to Psyche' is nevertheless pervaded by an air of calm and quiet. Cupid and Psyche are discovered lying motionless among '*hush'd*, cool-rooted flowers' and they are '*calm*-breathing'. In the final strophe the landscape is almost silent: trees merely 'murmur' in the wind, Dryads are 'lull'd to sleep' by low, gentle sounds, and the scene is described as a 'wide quietness'. 'Soft' is repeated three times in the poem, and it is noticeable how often Keats's ideal state of being includes these elements of silence, stillness, softness; for example, see also 'On the Sea', 'The Eve of St Agnes', 'Bright Star' and 'To Autumn'.

'Ode to a Nightingale'

(Written in May 1819; published in *Annals of the Fine Arts*, July 1819 and in *Poems*, 1820.)

According to Charles Brown, the 'Ode to a Nightingale' was written one spring morning in the garden of Wentworth Place, Hampstead. Apparently Keats took a chair on to the grass under a plum tree and, when he returned indoors two or three hours later, was seen to push a few scraps of paper behind some books. These scraps, Brown claimed, contained Keats's 'poetic feeling on the song of the nightingale'. What Brown saw was probably an early draft rather than the completed ode, but the anecdote (related many years after the event) sounds plausible because the ode has such an air of spontaneity and dramatic immediacy. Like a Shakespearean soliloquy it gives the effect of a profound, personal experience actually lived through within the space of its eighty lines. The poet himself dominates the poem; the word 'I' occurs in almost every stanza, and the poem opens and closes on a note of acute self-consciousness. At a first reading this ode appears to be a perfect example of Wordsworth's definition of poetry: 'the spontaneous overflow of powerful feelings'.

It should be remembered, however, that the nightingale, a bird whose song is heard chiefly at night, had been a traditional subject for poetry from the Middle Ages. In Classical legend the nightingale, or Philomel (literally, 'lover of song'), was a beautiful girl whom the gods turned into a bird after she had been raped and had her tongue cut out by her attacker; hence the association with melancholy and with unhappy love which figures in many poems about the nightingale. In 'Il Penseroso' (1632) Milton called the nightingale 'Most musical, most melancholy'. But both Wordsworth and Coleridge, in poems which Keats probably knew well, reversed the tradition of the melancholy nightingale and described its song as an exuberant outburst of joy. In 'O Nightingale' (1807) Wordsworth referred to its 'Tumultuous harmony and fierce!' And in 'The Nightingale: A Conversation Poem' the song reminded Coleridge that 'In Nature there is nothing melancholy' and seemed 'always full of love/And joyance' (1798). For them, as for many poets before them, the nightingale's song was a source of poetic inspiration and a stimulus to meditation on, for example, nature, love and mortality. So in making the apparent happiness of the nightingale's song the focus of his longing to escape from the world of human suffering, Keats is, characteristically, creating something individual and personal out of a long-established poetic tradition.

At the beginning of the ode the poet finds himself in a state of painful lethargy, almost as if he had taken poison or drugs and were sinking into unconsciousness. This is not caused by jealousy of the nightingale's happiness but (perhaps to the reader's surprise) by an excessive delight in the bird's song of approaching summer. In the second stanza he longs for wine, with its associations of Mediterranean sun and pleasure, to help him vanish with the nightingale into the darkness of the forest. In the third stanza he enumerates all that he would like to forget of the world's suffering: misery, illness, old age and premature death, the fading of beauty and the brevity of love. He urges himself onwards in his flight and, in the fourth stanza, reaches the nightingale with the aid, not of wine, but of poetic inspiration. Although there is a moon, little light filters through the dense foliage and he can identify the different woodland flowers by their scents alone. In stanza six, as the poet listens to the song of the nightingale in the enveloping darkness, he feels that this would be the perfect moment to achieve his previously-felt wish to die.

Stanza seven opens with a sudden leap of thought: the poet claims that the nightingale is a creature that does *not* die. Its song has been heard throughout the ages by rich and poor alike, by the exiled Ruth of the Bible and even round the deserted shores of fairyland. But the word 'forlorn' jolts him back to self-consciousness; imagination fails, the nightingale's song fades into the distance and the poet is left wondering whether his experience has been a vision or a mere daydream, and whether he is even now awake or asleep.

NOTES AND GLOSSARY:

aches . . . pains:	for intensity of pleasure felt as pain, see also 'aching Pleasure' in 'Ode on Melancholy'
hemlock:	a poisonous plant
Lethe:	in Classical mythology, the river running through Hades, the home of the dead; when drunk, its waters induced forgetfulness
Dryad:	in Classical mythology, a wood-nymph
Flora:	in Classical mythology, the goddess of flowers

Provençal song: song from a region in Southern France; this suggests both the grape harvest and the songs of the medieval troubadours, many of whom came from Provence

warm South: the Mediterranean climate

blushful Hippocrene: red wine; the Hippocrene fountain on Mount Helicon in Greece was a spring of water sacred to the Muses, hence the source of poetic inspiration. Wine as blushing water originates in the Bible story of Christ turning water into wine (St John, 2) but Keats may also be playing on the flushed cheeks caused by much drinking

youth grows pale...and dies: often taken to be a reference to Tom Keats, but the implication is probably more general

Bacchus and his pards: in Roman mythology, Bacchus was the god of wine and of poetic inspiration, usually represented riding in a chariot pulled by leopards

viewless: invisible

Fays: fairies; in this ode Keats mixes Classical deities with English fairies as Shakespeare does in *A Midsummer Night's Dream*

embalmed darkness: richly scented darkness, as with the aromatic drugs used to preserve a corpse. This suggests the heavy perfume of the flowers and anticipates the reference to death in stanza 6

eglantine: sweet-briar, or honeysuckle

Darkling: in the dark (archaic)

rich to die: magnificent to die at such an intense moment of experience. See also 'some rich anger' in 'Ode on Melancholy'

requiem: in the Christian Church, a service to pray for the soul of one recently dead; Keats imagines the bird's song to be a hymn for his own soul

clown: peasant; simple, uneducated person

Ruth: in the Bible story Ruth was driven into exile by famine and worked in the fields near Bethlehem

magic casements: see also the last lines of the 'Ode to Psyche'; Keats was very fond of windows looking out over water, such as a 'Window opening on Winander mere'

forlorn: lost, abandoned, neglected

bell...toll: slow, regular notes of a church bell rung at a funeral; this continues the imagery of death

the fancy cannot cheat so well: imagination cannot keep up the illusion (of the nightingale's immortality)

deceiving elf: imagination, personified as a mischievous sprite

plaintive anthem: as Keats's mood turns to regret, so the song appears sad; an anthem is a piece of music sung by a church choir, but Keats may be echoing Wordsworth's 'Solitary Reaper' (1807): 'Perhaps the plaintive numbers flow/For old, unhappy, far-off things,/And battles long ago ... '

Do I wake or sleep?: on the conflict between imagination and reality, vision and daydream, see the 'Ode to Psyche' and 'The Fall of Hyperion'

In March 1818 Keats had written in a verse-letter to John Hamilton Reynolds,

> It is a flaw
> In happiness to see beyond our bourn—
> It forces us in summer skies to mourn:
> It spoils the singing of the nightingale.

This realisation, that the wish to look beyond the normal limits of human happiness can destroy what pleasure the world has to offer, comes very close to what has been seen as the theme of this ode: the paradox that the world of the imagination offers a release from the painful world of actuality, but at the same time it renders the world of actuality more painful by contrast. The 'Ode to a Nightingale' dramatises the desire to lose oneself completely in a momentary experience of happiness. By an effort of the imagination Keats manages to subdue all his knowledge of human suffering and to enter so completely into the ecstasy of the nightingale's song that he becomes no more than an instrument recording the minutest particulars of physical sensation. He feels, for a moment, how marvellous it would be for his life to end in such a state of bliss. (Remember that many sixteenth- and seventeenth-century poets referred to the brief loss of consciousness after sex as 'the little death', so there is an erotic overtone at this point in the poem.) But death would mean the end, for Keats, of the nightingale's song. Now he makes another claim for the power of imagination over reality by asserting that the nightingale is immortal, and demonstrates that its song has been heard through historical and legendary time. But the fiction cannot be sustained, the bird flies out of earshot and the poet is returned, reluctantly and uncertainly, to reality.

The 'Ode to a Nightingale' is sometimes described as an escapist poem. It certainly alludes to a number of ways of avoiding reality, such as poison, narcotic drugs, wine, loss of memory, imagination and, finally, death itself. But a much stronger impulse is working in the poem, so that even while Keats is talking of drinking himself into oblivion, one image of light, warmth, energy and pleasure is piled on another so that the dominant mood is of vigorous, cheerful life. Notice the concentration of sense-impressions in stanza two, the refreshing coolness of wine intensified by 'sunburnt mirth' and 'the warm South', and the contrast between a sunlit, green landscape and the vivid close-up of 'beaded bubbles winking at the brim'. Keats substituted 'beaded' for 'cluster'd' in an earlier draft; ask yourself whether the change is an improvement, and if so, why? Contemporary critics objected to Keats's unorthodox imagery: how could wine *taste* of the green country, Flora, dance, song, etc? But nowadays this dense concentration of associations and images is regarded as one of the great achievements of the ode. Notice the unusual conjunction of sense-impressions in stanza four, 'light . . . with the breezes blown'. There is a similar synaesthetic image in stanza five: 'I cannot see . . . what soft incense hangs upon the boughs' suggests that the perfume is dense enough to be visible and tangible. If the poem is escapist, it is so only in that it is a flight from the misery and sickness of the world of men to the abundance and vigour of the world of nature. Among the fresh, heady scents of an English May woodland at night, the warmth of a Provençal grape harvest and a cornfield in the Middle East, the lure of death is a fleeting temptation; the ode celebrates above all the beauty and vigour of natural life.

'Ode on a Grecian Urn'

(Written in May 1819; published in the *Annals of the Fine Arts*, January 1820, and *Poems*, 1820.)

Urns, vase-like containers made of pottery or stone with rounded bodies and narrow necks, were used in ancient Greece and Rome to preserve the ashes of the dead. Many of these vessels, often beautifully decorated with painted or carved designs, survived in private collections or in public institutions, such as the British Museum. The urn to which this ode is addressed is less likely to be one particular example than an imaginary object, made up of details from many such urns or other works of art that Keats could have seen in museums or reproduced in books of engravings. For example, in stanza four the 'heifer lowing at the skies' may have been suggested by a fragment of the Elgin Marbles, part of the Parthenon frieze brought from Athens and exhibited in the British Museum. And the 'little town' in the same stanza could have been inspired by one of the pastoral landscapes by the French painter, Claude (1600–82), which Keats particularly admired.

In the early nineteenth century it was by no means unusual to make a work of painting or sculpture the subject of a poem. From 1810 to 1820 the subject of the Oxford University poetry competition had been a work of Classical sculpture or architecture. In his sonnet, 'Upon the Sight of a Beautiful Picture', (published in 1815) Wordsworth praised a work of art that could capture a moment of life and preserve it, unchanged, for ever, and give 'To one brief moment caught from fleeting time/The appropriate calm of blest eternity'. Wordsworth felt 'a peculiar satisfaction' in having anticipated Keats's thought in the 'Ode on a Grecian Urn', but he did not accuse Keats of borrowing the idea from his own poem. In its treatment of the relationship between imagination and reality, the temporal and the immortal, this ode is very close to the 'Ode to a Nightingale' although it is much less personal in tone; notice that the word 'I' does not appear at all in the poem.

Keats first questions the urn, personified as a bride of quietness, a child of time and a teller of pastoral tales, about the scenes decorating its sides. Are the figures humans or gods? What is this wild, amorous pursuit of reluctant maidens, resembling a Bacchanalian revel? In the second stanza the poet claims that the world pictured on the urn is superior to reality; its music is sweeter, its songs never-ending, and although the lover can never reach the girl he desires, she will always be beautiful and his love will never fade. In the third stanza he exclaims with mounting excitement at the happiness of this world of perpetual spring and music where lovers, forever in a blissful state of anticipation, are spared the disappointments and disillusion of mortal passion. In the fourth stanza a new scene arouses his curiosity: a priest leads a cow, garlanded with flowers, in procession to the sacrifice. This prompts the poet to wonder about the town from which they have come, left eternally devoid of inhabitants. The silent urn, with life frozen on its surface, is as perplexing as the idea of eternity. The only consolation the urn offers, as a work of art that outlasts human lives, is the single thought, that beauty and truth are one and the same.

NOTES AND GLOSSARY:

still unravished bride: the urn is unbroken, intact, as a virgin is sexually intact; 'still' can be read as an adjective, meaning 'motionless', or as an adverb, meaning 'as yet' or 'so far'

foster-child: as the urn's maker, its parent, is dead, it has been cared for by time and silence

Sylvan: woodland (Latin: *silva*, a wood)

historian: the urn describes a series of events through the pictures which decorate it

Tempe: a valley in ancient Greece celebrated for its beautiful, cool woodlands

Arcadia: a mountainous region of Greece, described by the Roman poet, Virgil (70–19 BC), as an earthly paradise, the home of shepherds and their god, Pan

loth: reluctant
mad pursuit: wild, excited pursuit; this scene of a frenzied sexual chase is characteristic of the ritual worship of Bacchus (Dionysus), god of wine, and a common subject for decoration of a vase or urn
ditties of no tone: songs inaudible to the human ear
Attic: from Athens in ancient Greece, therefore Classically simple in form
brede: interwoven decorative border
overwrought: painted or carved on the surface
tease us out of thought: either, 'frustrate our attempts to think reasonably' or 'jolt us out of mere, dull reasoning'. See the verse-letter to J.H. Reynolds (March 1818): 'Things cannot to the will/Be settled, but they tease us out of thought'
Pastoral: a story of the idealised, country life of Arcadian shepherds (Latin: *pastor*, a shepherd). The poetic tradition of pastoral originated with the Greek, Theocritus (third century BC), who was later imitated by Virgil
When old age ... waste: when everyone now living has died of old age
"Beauty is truth, truth beauty,"—that is all/Ye know on earth, and all ye need to know: these lines have always caused a major problem of interpretation, largely because uncertainty over punctuation makes it unclear who speaks these lines. It is likely that 'Beauty is truth, truth beauty', is the kind of moral sentiment sometimes inscribed on such urns, and the remainder the reassuring 'voice' of the urn itself. (The lines quoted here are as printed in *Poems*, 1820)

The 'Ode on a Grecian Urn' deals dramatically with the paradox that a work of art that is silent, motionless, made of cold marble and, by its very function, associated with death, can suggest a world of warmth, colour, music, vitality and passionate feeling. This paradox is summed up in the phrase, 'Cold Pastoral', and there are other examples of such apparent self-contradictions in the poem, as 'Heard melodies are sweet, but those unheard/Are sweeter' and 'ditties of no tone'. Puns, such as 'Attic ... attitude', and ambiguities, such as the play on 'still' in the first line, illustrate the mysterious, indefinable nature of the relationship between life and art. (Notice how the double meaning of 'still' is repeated in 'For ever warm and still to be enjoy'd'.) The number of questions the poet addresses to the urn and the figures on it shows how convincingly real the world pictured on the urn seems to be; so real that the poet is led to imagine a 'little town', not figured on the urn, from which the procession has come, leaving the town forever empty and silent.

Critical discussion of this ode has tended to concentrate on the last two lines. Even if we take 'Beauty is truth, truth beauty' to be a quasi-philosophical statement uttered by the urn, and the following words to be a spontaneous message of reassurance also spoken by the urn, we are still left with a problem: what does this mean? This has been extensively debated, and the general feeling is that these two final lines offer too glib and facile a solution to the mystery Keats has dramatised so vividly in the ode. It is clear from his letters that Keats had for some time been preoccupied with the relationship between beauty (that is, the idealising quality of a work of art) and truth (that is, the inescapable facts of reality) although he knew he lacked the philosophical knowledge and training to deal with these concepts. In November 1817 he had written to Benjamin Bailey, 'What the imagination seizes as Beauty must be truth—whether it existed before or not— .... The Imagination may be compared to Adam's dream—he awoke and found it truth.' And later in the same year he wrote to his brothers, 'The excellence of every Art is its intensity, capable of making all disagreeables evaporate, from their being in close relationship with Beauty & Truth.' And in the long letter to George Keats which ran from December 1818 to January 1819, 'I never can feel certain of any truth but from a clear perception of its Beauty.' If we can accept that life and art are equally real and beautiful, we are nevertheless left puzzling over the idea that this is *all* we need to know, and how this emerges from the previous four stanzas of the poem.

'Ode on Melancholy'

(Written in May 1819; published in *Poems*, 1820.)

Melancholy was once known as 'the Elizabethan malady' and one of Keats's favourite texts was a treatise on its causes, symptoms, cure and social implications, *The Anatomy of Melancholy*, by Robert Burton (1577–1640), published in 1621. Shakespeare and his contemporaries were interested in the condition, and Hamlet is often regarded as a typical example of the melancholy man, solitary, thoughtful, tending to doubt and inactivity, alternating despair with bouts of false laughter, and finding the beauties of the world veiled by 'a foul and pestilent congregation of vapours'. Keats may well have been reading Burton in the spring of 1819, for his attitude echoes Burton's own: melancholy is an integral part of experience and must be accepted willingly as an inevitable element in life. In March Keats had written to George and Georgiana:

This is the world—thus we cannot expect to give way many hours to pleasure—While we are laughing the seed of some trouble is put into the wide arable land of events—while we are laughing it sprouts grows and suddenly bears a poison fruit which we must pluck.

Keats was well aware of his own tendency to 'horrid Morbidity'; what he called melancholy we might now describe as depression, an illness which can lead to acts as well as thoughts of suicide in its acute form.

In this ode Keats does not address his subject, Melancholy, directly, but instead makes a plea to an unnamed listener (rather as he does in the sestet of the sonnet, 'On the Sea'). The poem opens with an urgent, emphatic command not to seek oblivion or resort to poison, and not to indulge in thoughts of graveyards or other reminders of death. Such things will obliterate all feeling, and consciousness of pain is better than no consciousness at all. In the second stanza he tells the sufferer, when melancholy overwhelms you, feed it to the point of satiety by looking at fresh, beautiful flowers, the sunlit spray of a wave breaking, or the light in your mistress's eyes when she is angry. In stanza three Keats explains, through the device of personification, that melancholy is inseparable from beauty that is impermanent, from fleeting moments of happiness and from the kind of pleasure that turns to bitterness even while it is enjoyed. The goddess, Melancholy, has her shrine in the temple sacred to Delight, but only the man capable of experiencing the most acute happiness can see her face to face; only he can appreciate her mournful power and be counted among her worshippers.

NOTES AND GLOSSARY:

Lethe: see note on 'Ode to a Nightingale', p.48

Wolf's-bane: aconite, a poisonous plant

nightshade: plant with poisonous red berries (hence 'ruby grape')

Proserpine: in Classical mythology, the daughter of Zeus and Demeter, goddess of harvest; she was compelled to spend six months of the year in the underworld as the consort of Pluto, ruler of the dead, but was allowed to return to earth each spring

yew-berries: poisonous berries of an evergreen tree, often grown in churchyards

death-moth: the death's head hawk-moth, so called because of its skull-like markings

Psyche: see note on the 'Ode to Psyche', p.43

sorrow's mysteries: ritual worship in honour of the goddess, Melancholy

shade to shade: a play on a double meaning: the shadow of death will fall on the soul

shroud: the cloth in which a corpse is wrapped for burial, hence a concealing drapery

glut: literally, feed until the stomach is over-full. The meaning here is ambiguous: either, intensify your sorrow with images of short-lived beauty, or, overcome your sorrow by reminding yourself of the beauty and vitality of the world. (See Shakespeare's *Twelfth Night*, Act I, scene 1: 'If music be the food of love, play on;/Give me excess of it, that surfeiting,/The appetite may sicken, and so die.')

globed peonies: flower that has a spherical bud and a cup-shaped, many-petalled bloom

some rich anger...eyes: relish the magnificent vitality of your mistress's anger. See Keats's letter of 14 February–3 May 1819: 'Though a quarrel in the streets is a thing to be hated, the energies displayed in it are fine; the commonest Man shows a grace in his quarrel.'

She dwells with Beauty: 'She' is the goddess, Melancholy, not the mistress of the previous stanza

aching Pleasure: the apparently paradoxical association of pleasure and pain is a theme common to the Spring odes. There is probably a suggestion of sexual pleasure here; when sensation is extreme and intense pleasure and pain are almost indistinguishable

whose strenuous tongue/Can burst Joy's grape: a powerfully physical image, suggesting that the experience of happiness is primarily sensual

cloudy trophies: memorials of victory in battle, such as armour or banners, were displayed in Classical temples and also in English churches

The 'Elizabethan malady' of melancholy was sometimes affected as a pose by people with a cynical, world-weary attitude. For example, in Shakespeare's *As You Like It* 'the melancholy Jaques' turns the sight of a wounded deer abandoned by the herd into an opportunity to brood on man's inhumanity to man. His sadness seems more contrived than genuine and he confesses that it is 'a melancholy of mine own, compounded of many simples [ingredients]'. In a cancelled first stanza of this ode Keats seems to be addressing such a person, who is consciously searching for something to make himself melancholy. Keats emphasises that ghoulish thoughts of Gothic horrors are not the means to experience true melancholy, and this line of argument is continued in the first stanza of the completed ode. The 'goddess Melancholy' is not found in the macabre and the morbid; 'she' is revealed to the man of extreme sensitivity who can feel the sadness of fading beauty and fleeting happiness.

Closely linked as it is to the 'Ode to a Nightingale' and the 'Ode on a Grecian Urn', this ode differs from each of the other two in tone. It is less personal than the Nightingale ode (the word 'I' does not appear in this poem), more didactic than the 'Ode on a Grecian Urn'. The emotional charge is generated, not by the poet's direct expressions of feeling, but by the strangely paradoxical instructions and imagery of the second stanza.

In stanza two the simile for melancholy is itself paradoxical; the April shower is both 'weeping' and like a 'shroud', but it is also life-giving in that it revives the drooping flowers. The unpleasant image, 'glut', with its associations of greed and lust, is attached to images of beauty and freshness. The 'morning' rose is probably a newly-opened bud still covered with dew, and the breaking wave holds for an instant the colours of the rainbow in its blown spray. But the final image of the stanza has puzzled and even angered critics; 'feeding' upon one's mistress's eyes while indifferent to her anger suggests perverse aestheticism or even sadism. However, the thought is likely to be that of the letter quoted in the Notes and Glossary above: what is admirable is the energy displayed in a passing fit of anger.

The tension between pleasure and pain is sustained in the personifications of the final stanza; 'aching Pleasure' and Joy forever bidding farewell are reinforced by another vivid but enigmatic image of the fleeting moment. 'Turning to poison while the bee-mouth sips' may suggest either pleasure turning to bitterness in the few seconds it takes for a bee to extract nectar from a flower, or the equally instantaneous conversion of the sweet nectar to the poison of the bee's sting. The final image of the sensuality of happiness, of happiness described as the act of eating, is clear, unambiguous and almost shocking in its physicality. Keats continues his allegorical quest in 'The Fall of Hyperion' where the melancholy goddess appears as Moneta (memory) and the poet is allowed to see her face to face.

'To Autumn'

(Written in September 1819; published in *Poems*, 1820.)

'To Autumn' was composed soon after Keats had been out for a walk one evening in the fields near Winchester, an old cathedral town in the South of England. This extract from a letter dated 21 September 1819 to J.H. Reynolds shows how many of the details in the poem were drawn from Keats's recent experience:

How beautiful the season is now—How fine the air. A temperate sharpness about it. Really, without joking, chaste weather—Dian skies—I never lik'd stubble fields so much as now—Aye better than the chilly green of the spring. Somehow a stubble plain looks warm —in the same way that some pictures look warm—this struck me so much in my sunday's walk that I compos'd upon it.

The reference to 'Dian', or Diana, shows how spontaneously Keats's knowledge and love of Classical myth and legend formed part of his response to the beauty of nature. Diana, goddess of the moon and of chastity, was also a huntress, preferring the excitement of the chase to the delights of love. Although she herself does not appear in the poem, there is a hint of a benign, supernatural presence in the Autumn who 'conspires' with the sun in stanza 1, and in the four personifications of Autumn in stanza 2. Also, while the landscape of the poem is undeniably English, the figures in stanza 2 are reminiscent of Ceres, goddess of harvest, and their placing in the landscape recalls the paintings of Poussin (1593/4−1665), a French artist admired by Keats.

In the first stanza Keats addresses Autumn, who collaborates with the sun in the process of bringing fruit and nuts to ripeness and who also provides late-flowering blossoms so that the bees can continue to fill their brimming honeycombs. The second stanza opens with a rhetorical question which calls on the reader's own experience: surely we have all caught sight of Autumn, either resting in a grain-filled barn, asleep among the wheat, carrying a head-load of corn across a stream, or watching the slow run of juice from a cider-press? In the third stanza the remembered sounds of spring are dismissed in favour of the distinctive music of autumn; sunset brings the faint sounds of clouds of insects, the bleat of lambs on the hillsides and the characteristic notes of the robin and flocks of swallows.

NOTES AND GLOSSARY:

bosom-friend: intimate friend

maturing: a double meaning is possible: getting older as the year passes, and bringing crops to ripeness

thatch-eves: overhanging edges of roofs made of straw or reeds

o'er-brimm'd: filled to overflowing

clammy: moist and sticky (because filled with honey)

careless: either, free of care (because the harvest is safely gathered), or physically relaxed

Drows'd with the fume of poppies: the wild English field poppy with its bright red flower was a common sight in cornfields before the use of modern weedkillers; it has very little scent, so Keats is probably thinking of the narcotic derived from the opium poppy

swath: the amount of standing corn that can be cut with one stroke of a scythe or reaping-hook

gleaner: a field-worker who picks up stalks of wheat or other grain dropped when the corn is gathered into sheaves. (In the Bible story Ruth gleaned in the fields owned by Boaz)

cyder-press: a machine for extracting apple juice to make an alcoholic drink. Devon, which Keats visited, is still famous for its cider

bloom: Keats's use of the word as a verb is unusual; it suggests shedding a warm, hazy light

wailful choir . . . mourn: the faint sound made by the insects' wings has a mournful effect, but Keats may also be suggesting that they are lamenting the dying of the year

sallows: willow trees

hilly bourn: hills bounding the horizon

Hedge-cricket: an invention of Keats's own; the cricket is an insect whose chirping sound is heard chiefly in winter

red-breast: the robin, a bird with a distinctive red breast often seen in British gardens; its melodious whistling song is a common winter sound

gathering swallows: swallows congregate in large numbers before they migrate south in the autumn

Many English people prefer the so-called 'Indian Summer' of mid-September to any other time of year. It is a phase in the seasons when the landscape can be particularly beautiful as the trees are still in full green leaf, while many fields are golden with the straw-stubble left after the harvest. While the early mornings can be cool and misty there is still a great deal of warmth in the sun at mid-day, and there is often a welcome lull in the weather between the thunderstorms characteristic of late August and the gales that begin in early October. This short ode is a wonderfully vivid evocation of the characteristic sights, sounds and atmosphere of the English rural landscape in this brief season. The mood of the poem is one of serene satisfaction; the flux of time which was such a terrifying and destructive force in the Spring odes is here slowed almost to a standstill. (In the second stanza nothing moves except the hair blown by the wind and the slow drip of juice from the cider-press.) Hints of the past spring and the coming winter arouse neither regret nor fear. The gnats may emit a melancholy sound, but the final image of the swallows gathering for their autumn migration reminds us that the process of the seasons is cyclical. The swallows must depart in autumn but they will also return in the following spring. There is no explicit thought or philosophy in the poem; the poet does not interpose an obtrusive 'I' between the reader and the images of the rural landscape. The reassurance, that while this moment of perfection must pass it will also return, is implicit in the nature of Keats's imagery. The tone of this ode has been described as Shakespearean and in it Keats has certainly achieved an air of calm detachment; it is much less an expression of 'I feel' than a demonstration of 'This is how it is.'

This ode has been widely celebrated for the wealth and concentration of its imagery. F.R. Leavis spoke of its 'sensuous richness . . . without the least touch of artistic over-ripeness'. Notice in stanza 1 how much energy and vitality is packed into the series of monosyllabic verbs, all suggesting activity: 'load', 'bless', 'run', 'bend', 'fill', 'swell', 'plump', 'set'. Read the stanza aloud and notice its vigorous, emphatic effect, then continue with stanza 2 and feel the change in the texture of the language: it relaxes and softens just as the subject-matter shifts from action to relaxation. A subtle pattern of assonance and alliteration contributes to this effect. Notice the echoes in 'soft-lifted by the winnowing wind', 'Drows'd . . . flowers . . . hours by hours'. Keats achieves a concentration of meaning by inventing new compound words such as 'cottage-trees', 'soft-lifted', 'soft-dying', 'stubble-plains'. And another innovation in this ode is the addition of an extra, eleventh line to the stanza he had evolved in the earlier odes. It is difficult to define the precise effect of this extension; what it does mean is that, while the rhyme scheme of the opening quatrain remains unchanged (*a b a b*), the pattern of the remaining seven lines is more complex and takes longer to resolve. All three stanzas end with a rhyming couplet followed by a rhyme echoing the seventh line of the stanza, a strangely delayed echo which has a somewhat haunting effect. Altogether 'To Autumn' is an astonishing achievement and there are those who regard it as, if not his greatest, then certainly Keats's most perfectly achieved poem.

'Lamia'

(Part I written in June and July, Part II in August and September 1819; printed in *Poems*, 1820.)

In Classical mythology a lamia was a monster, half woman and half serpent, who lured strangers (especially children) into her clutches and then devoured them. Keats discovered the story on which this poem is based in Book III of Robert Burton's *Anatomy of Melancholy*, where Burton referred to the Pythagorean philosopher, Apollonius (first century AD), whose wisdom was reputedly able to overcome witchcraft. 'Lamia' is in effect an extended version of the story 'La Belle Dame sans Merci': a man falls prey to the charms of a beautiful, supernatural creature but, after a brief period of bliss, their love ends unhappily.

In this poem Keats returns to the Classical world of myth and legend; the setting is exotic and the sensuous richness of the 'palace of sweet sin' in Part II almost overwhelming in its luxuriance. It must be remembered that in the summer of 1819 Keats was desperately anxious to make money; in the gap between composing Parts I and II of 'Lamia' he was working with Charles Brown on 'Otho the Great', the tragedy they hoped would make them rich and famous. Keats was deliberately setting out to appeal to his readers' taste for excitement by composing a verse tale of exotic mystery. In September he wrote to his brother and sister-in-law,

> I have been reading over a part of a short poem I have composed lately call'd 'Lamia'—and I am certain there is that sort of fire in it which must take hold of people in some way—give them either pleasant or unpleasant sensation. What they want is a sensation of some sort.

It was probably the hope that 'Lamia' would 'take hold' of its readers that inspired Keats to have it printed as the first poem in the collection published in 1820.

Two aspects of the poem deserve particular attention in your first readings. As well as following the details of the strange story, notice the effects of the form Keats has chosen. 'Lamia' is written in heroic couplets: what is the effect of the long series of very obvious couplet rhymes? And notice, too, the attitude of the narrator to his story, remembering how closely and sympathetically the narrator was involved with the characters and events of 'The Eve of St Agnes'. After he had completed Part I of the poem in July Keats wrote, 'I have great hopes of success, because I made use of my Judgement more deliberately than I yet have done.' Do you see any signs of increased 'judgement' in this poem?

Part I, lines 1–170

Long ago, when the gods of Olympus still reigned supreme, the god Hermes descended to Crete in search of the nymph with whom he had fallen passionately in love. While resting from his long and fruitless search he heard a sad voice bewailing its fate, and discovered the speaker to be an extraordinary creature, snake-like in form but with the beautiful eyes and mouth of a woman and a woman's voice as well. The creature claimed to know of Hermes' quest, and promised to restore his nymph to him if he in return would enable her to change back into her proper shape as a woman. Hermes made the promise, the nymph appeared and, after violent and agonising convulsions, the snake shed its brilliant skin and a lady emerged, calling the name of her lover, Lycius.

NOTES AND GLOSSARY:

before the faery broods...: before the native English supernatural creatures supplanted the ancient Greek divinities

Satyr: in Classical myth a follower of Dionysus, a male spirit with the legs and hoofs of a goat, traditionally boisterous and lustful

Oberon: king of the fairies in Shakespeare's *A Midsummer Night's Dream*

Dryad: a wood-nymph

Faun: similar to a Satyr

ever-smitten Hermes: Hermes, the messenger of the gods of Olympus, was famous for his many love-affairs

Tritons: in Classical myth, sea-gods, half men and half fish

wither'd: the Tritons soon shrivel up when out of the water

cirque-couchant: lying in circular coils (a term invented by Keats from the language of heraldry)

gordian: intricately entwined; from the knot of Gordius, who tied the yoke to the pole of his waggon so tightly that no one could undo it. (Alexander the Great cut it with his sword and fulfilled the prophecy that the knot would be untied by the future ruler of Asia)

Eyed like a peacock: covered with patterns like the eye-shaped designs on a peacock's tail

penanced lady elf: fairy suffering the punishment of being turned into an animal

the demon's self: in the Bible story the Devil, or Satan, appeared to Eve in the Garden of Eden disguised as a snake, or serpent

Ariadne's tiar: in Classical myth Dionysus (Bacchus), god of wine, loved Ariadne and gave her a crown which after her death became a constellation of seven stars

Proserpine: see note on 'Ode to Melancholy': her home on earth was the Mediterranean island of Sicily

Like a stoop'd falcon: like the bird of prey that is about to drop suddenly on its victim

Apollo: Greek god of music and poetry

robed in purple flakes: clothed in mist or cloud coloured purple by the sunrise; as in 'The Eve of St Agnes', purple is associated with passion

Phoebean dart: sunbeam, literally an arrow shot by Phoebus, god of the sun

star of Lethe: Hermes; he escorted the souls of the dead across Lethe, the river of forgetfulness, to the underworld

blear'd Silenus:	an elderly, drunken Satyr; fat, jolly and lecherous
Circean:	like the sorceress, Circe, who had the power to turn men into animals
the lythe Caducean charm:	as a token of his office as messenger, Hermes carried a Caduceus, a short staff entwined with two snakes, which he used to cast spells
besprent:	sprinkled (archaic)
brede:	see note on 'Ode on a Grecian urn', p.53
rubious-argent:	literally, reddish-silver (a term invented by Keats from the language of heraldry)

Part I, lines 171–397

Now transformed into a beautiful woman, Lamia appeared in a valley near Corinth, in Greece. The narrator exclaims at Lycius's luck, for, while still a virgin, Lamia possesses all the knowledge and skill of an experienced lover. When she was a serpent she had the power to travel in imagination all over the world and, having seen Lycius and fallen in love with him, she was now waiting for him to pass by along the Corinth road. Engrossed in thought, he did not notice her at first, but when she greeted him and he saw how beautiful she was, he fell instantly in love with her and begged her never to leave him. Lamia, sure of her power over Lycius, pretended to be a divine creature, unable to survive on earth, and at this news Lycius fainted. Gloating at her hold over him, Lamia revived Lycius and assured him that she was a real woman of Corinth. Together they went to the city, Lycius unaware of the magical speed of their journey, and made their way through the crowded, torchlit streets. Lycius concealed himself in particular from one grey-bearded, sharp-eyed old man they passed and admitted to Lamia that this was his former tutor, Apollonius, who had once seemed so wise and trustworthy but now seemed no more than a ghost of past foolishness. Then they crossed the marble threshold of doorway whose gates opened to the sound of music and entered a house invisible to anyone else in Corinth. Here the narrator breaks off, but hints that bad news will follow this apparently happy ending.

NOTES AND GLOSSARY:

Cenchreas:	the port of Corinth in Greece. These geographical details appeared in Burton's version of the story
Cleone:	village on the road from Corinth to Argos
passioned:	verb invented by Keats, probably meaning 'expressed passionate delight'
Spread a green kirtle . . . :	sat with her green skirts spread around her while she listened . . .
sciential:	endowed with knowledge, ability

To unperplex bliss from its neighbour pain: the predominating theme of the Spring odes, especially the 'Ode on Melancholy'

unshent: unsullied, unspoilt (archaic); Lamia is still a virgin although she is a 'graduate' in the arts of love

Elysium: in Classical mythology, the home of virtuous souls after death, paradise

Nereids: sea-nymphs

Thetis: a sea-nymph, mother of the hero Achilles

glutinous: sticky with resin

palatine: palatial, extensive

Mulciber: Roman god of fire, also known as Vulcan, maker of the armour of the gods

piazzian: like the colonnade surrounding an open square or piazza

Jove heard his vows: Jupiter (Jove), the Roman equivalent of Zeus, king and father of the gods, had special care of marriage

Platonic shades: thoughts of the Greek philosopher, Plato (c. 427–348 BC)

syllabling: speaking softly (see Milton's *Comus*, line 208, 'Airy tongues, that syllable men's names')

Orpheus-like at an Eurydice: in the Classical legend the poet, Orpheus, was promised that he might rescue his beloved Eurydice from the underworld provided that he did not look behind him to see if she was following. He could not resist the temptation to look, and lost her for ever

Pleaid: one of the seven stars of the constellation, the Pleiades; in legend, the daughters of Atlas, who were turned into stars after death

keep in tune/Thy spheres: refers to the theory of the Greek mathematician and philosopher, Pythagoras (sixth century BC), who believed that the cosmic system was earth-centred and that the moon, sun, planets and stars revolved around it fixed in their concentric spheres, which emitted harmonious music. Lycius imagines Lamia to be a star fallen from the sky and asks whether one of her sisters can replace her so that she does not have to leave him

My essence: the ethereal element of which gods are made, as opposed to mortal clay

amenity: compliance, agreeableness

subtle fluid: rarified, ethereal liquid

Adonian feast:	festival sacred to Adonis, the youth loved in legend by the goddess Venus, celebrated annually as a fertility rite. (Lamia is lying; we know she has dreamed of Lycius in a chariot race, but the reference to the passionate love of Venus and Adonis suits her much better)
Peris:	in Persian myth, good fairies in the shape of beautiful sylphs
Pyrrha's pebbles:	in Greek myth Deucalion and his wife, Pyrrha, re-peopled the world after a great flood by throwing into the water pebbles, which then emerged as human beings; Deucalion's became men and Pyrrha's became women
Adam's seed:	in the Bible Adam is the first man and the father of the human race
comprized:	completely absorbed
lewd:	either in the obsolete sense of 'common', 'vulgar', or 'lascivious', 'licentious', referring to the sexual acts performed during the festival of Adonis
Apollonius:	a philosopher from Asia Minor, famous also for his magical powers. Burton quoted the story of Apollonius's encounter with Lycius and a lamia from a biography by Philostratus (born 170 AD) and Keats had the extract printed in *Poems*, 1820
Aeolian:	like the sound of a wind-harp, called after Aeolus, Greek god of the winds and storms
flitter-winged:	light-winged
And but . . . incredulous:	'If the light-winged verse did not have to tell, in order to be truthful, what unhappiness followed, it would please many people to leave the lovers here, secluded from the busy world, and to imagine no more about them.' As narrator, Keats is adopting a deliberately unsentimental attitude here

Part II, lines 1—145

Love lasts neither for rich nor for poor, the narrator remarks drily, but Lycius lived for too short a time to prove or disprove this saying, although the god of love himself watched closely over the lovers. One evening as they were lying together Lycius was suddenly reminded of the world outside their secluded palace and the lady, sensing that Lycius's attention had wandered, accused him of wanting to leave her. He swore that, on the contrary, he longed to make their love public and to present her to Corinth as his bride. The lady, obviously distressed by this idea, wept and begged Lycius to change his mind, but her tears only made him more brutally determined to have his own way and eventually she, enjoying his tyranny, submitted. The lady (who still had not told Lycius her name) claimed to have neither friends nor family living, and so had no one to invite to the wedding, but she begged Lycius not to include Apollonius among the guests and refused to give him a reason.

While Lycius went out to deliver invitations the bride made her preparations for the ceremony she dreaded but could not escape. With the aid of mysterious, invisible helpers and to the sound of strange music she transformed the palace hall into an elaborate arbour; an aisle of lamplit trees ran down the centre with a lavish feast laid beneath them. When she had supervised all the final details Lamia disappeared to await the unwelcome intrusion of the guests.

NOTES AND GLOSSARY:

non-elect: literally, those whom God has not rewarded with eternal life after death; here, those who have not experienced the pains and pleasures of love

given the moral a fresh frown: given the maxim a new slant or meaning

clench'd: clinched, proved

Love, jealous grown . . . : ambiguous: either, Cupid is anxiously protective (in the archaic sense of 'jealous'), or he is envious of the lovers' bliss. The 'fearful roar' of his wings could be either threatening or protective

For all this: despite all this

tythe: tithe, a tenth; here, a small part, a fraction

purple-lined palace of sweet sin: purple is the colour of royal splendour and of passionate love (see also 'The Eve of St Agnes). Their love may be a 'sin' because they are not married, or because there is something evil and unnatural about it

silver planet: Venus, the morning and evening star, named after the goddess of love

he took delight/Luxurious: he luxuriated in, or took intense pleasure in

like Apollo's presence . . . serpent: in Classical legend the infant god Apollo killed Python, a monstrous serpent that had emerged from the mud after the flood of Deucalion

certes: certainly (archaic)

She burnt, she lov'd the tyranny: Keats himself commented, 'Women love to be forced to do a thing, by a fine fellow— *such as this* . . . '

Missioned: commissioned, ordered

fretted: elaborately carved

Part II, lines 146–311

On the wedding-day a horde of guests arrived (and the narrator reproaches Lycius for his foolishness in flaunting his private happiness in public). The guests marvelled at the house they had never noticed before in the familiar street, but there was one who showed no surprise. This was Apollonius, who merely chuckled as if he had just solved a tricky problem. He apologised for appearing uninvited and allowed the embarassed Lycius to lead him in to the banquet.

The banquet-hall was a brilliant sight, perfumed with incense, richly carpeted, and set with tables bearing golden drinking vessels and an abundance of food and wine. The guests, duly washed, robed and anointed, took their seats, wondering who was responsible for this lavish hospitality. But as music played and the wine flowed the conversation grew louder and more uninhibited. Garlands of leaves and flowers were brought for the guests to wear, and the narrator wonders ironically what might be suitable for Lamia, Lycius and for the philosopher, Apollonius, whose cold reason reduces all the mysterious beauties of nature to dull facts, just as it once turned Lamia into a ghost.

On turning to drink a toast to his old tutor, Lycius found that Apollonius was staring fixedly at Lamia, and Lycius felt his bride's hand turn unnaturally hot and cold. To his horror, he found that Lamia had become both blind and dumb, and the whole company fell silent at Lycius's cry of terror. He cursed Apollonius, accusing him of exercising demonic powers, but the philosopher retorted contemptuously that, on the contrary, it was he who had saved Lycius from the demonic power of a serpent. On hearing this word Lamia shuddered as if she had been stabbed, and, as he repeated, 'serpent', with a terrible scream she vanished. And when they reached the couch where he lay, the guests found that Lycius, too, was dead.

NOTES AND GLOSSARY:

daft: daffed (dialect): teased, resisted

sphered tables ... insphered: according to some historians the Greeks made tables spherical in imitation of the shape of the world; as the tables are surrounded ('insphered') by seats, Keats probably means 'circular'

libbard's: leopard's (archaic). In ancient Greece and Rome furniture was often made with legs in the shape of animals' limbs and feet

Ceres' horn: Ceres, the Greek goddess of harvest, is often represented with a huge cornucopia or 'horn of plenty', out of which pours a profusion of fruit, vegetables and sheaves of corn

sweet wine,/Will make Elysian shades not too fair: wine makes Heaven seem less far away and unattainable

osier'd: woven, like the pliable twigs of the osier or willow, often used for basket making

willow: tree with long, narrow leaves that grows by water, traditionally associated with sorrow

adder's tongue: fern with leaves shaped like the tongue of a species of snake (hence its suitability for Lamia)

thyrsus: staff carried by Bacchus, god of wine, entwined with vine-leaves and ivy (which has a poisonous berry)

Philosophy will clip an Angel's wings: philosophy here is natural philosophy, or what we would call science. At a dinner-party given by Haydon in 1817 Keats had agreed with Charles Lamb that the scientist, Sir Isaac Newton (1642–1727), had 'destroyed all the poetry of the rainbow' by reducing it to the spectrum of colours produced by light passing through a glass prism

gnomed mine: in popular folklore, gnomes, supernatural dwarf-like creatures, were believed to live underground and dig for precious stones

deep-recessed vision: suggests that Lamia's eyes are both sunken and blankly unfocused

juggling: conjuring, bewitching

sophist: teacher of philosophy and rhetoric

perceant: piercing (a Spenserian archaism)

'Lamia', the fourth and last of Keats's narrative poems on the theme of passionate love, leaves quite a different impression on the reader from the earlier 'Endymion', 'Isabella' and 'The Eve of St Agnes'. In these three poems the attitude to love and lovers was unequivocal, whereas 'Lamia' leaves the reader wondering where his or her sympathies should lie: with Lamia, who at first seemed a pathetic victim of evil enchantment, but who later proves cruel and deceitful herself and, later still, is subject to Lycius's tyranny? Or should the reader sympathise with Lycius, first the innocent object of Lamia's desire but later an unpleasant bully as well as a devoted lover? Or are we to approve of Apollonius, who with the penetrating eye of reason attempts to save Lycius from the snares of enchantment, but only at the cost of his erstwhile pupil's death? In Keats's source, Burton's *Anatomy of Melancholy*, the story was much more straightforward: an innocent young man was rescued from the enchantment of a lamia through the insight of a wise philosopher. The death of Lycius and the ambiguity of Apollonius's role were Keats's own additions, and they make the poem more sensational and more complicated than the original source.

From the vigour of the writing and the many passages of richly detailed description it appears that Keats revelled in the sensationalism of his subject-matter. You will have noticed the sinister brilliance of Lamia as a serpent (Part I, lines 47–67), her violent and grotesque metamorphosis into human form (Part I, lines 146–70), and, in Part II, the magical preparation of the banqueting-hall (lines 117–45). But Keats also shows an increased interest in the dramatic potential of the power-games typical of a passionately possessive love-relationship. In Part I Lamia dominates, 'without any show/Of sorrow for her tender favourite's woe', revelling in the power that keeps Lycius 'so tangled in her mesh'. The power shifts in Part II and here it Lycius who exerts his will, discovering a perverse pleasure in Lamia's unhappiness; 'Against his better self, he took delight/Luxurious in her sorrows, soft and new'. But now Lamia finds a new pleasure in his assertiveness; 'She burnt, she lov'd the tyranny', a sure indication, the narrator comments, that she is a *real* woman. While he was writing 'Lamia' Keats was himself experiencing the pains and the delights of a passionate love-affair. In July he wrote to Fanny Brawne from the Isle of Wight, 'Ask yourself my love whether you are not very cruel to have so entrammelled me, so destroyed my freedom', and a few weeks later, 'You absorb me in spite of myself.' Lamia and Lycius may long for an ideal love, but they are certainly not presented as ideal lovers; Keats's psychological accuracy is more honest than flattering. And in his role as narrator, Keats, speaking in a cynical, world-weary voice reminiscent of the tone of Lord Byron's (1788–1824) *Don Juan* (1819–24), repeatedly reminds his readers how often and how far human experience falls short of perfection. The opening episode of Hermes and the nymph serves, too, to emphasise that only the gods may expect to have all their desires completely satisfied.

Keats's verse form in this poem is the 'heroic couplet', that is, lines of iambic pentameter rhyming *a a b b*, etc. The form was introduced to England by Geoffrey Chaucer (c. 1345–1400) who used it for many of his *Canterbury Tales*, and it acquired the description, 'heroic', in the late seventeenth century through its use by many tragic and epic dramatists. John Dryden (1631–1700) was Keats's chief model, who, with Alexander Pope (1688–1744) helped to establish the heroic couplet as the chief poetic form in eighteenth-century England. Keats had used the form for 'Endymion', but his handling of it in 'Lamia' is much tighter, brisker and less rambling. Generally he maintains a steady flow of narrative, allowing the sense to over-run the couplet rhyme and thus avoiding the braking effect of the closed couplet (that is, when the end of a couplet coincides with the completion of a unit of sense). Chiefly because of the work of Alexander Pope the heroic couplet has become associated with satire and there are occasions in 'Lamia', especially in the narrator's asides to the reader, when Keats exploits the humorous quality of rhyme, as, for example,

> Love in a hut, with water and a crust,
> Is—Love, forgive us!—cinders, ashes, dust.

These authorial comments are a curious feature of the poem; their tone is often sardonic, world-weary and strangely at odds with the violent and fantastic events of the story. Contemporary critics found some of the remarks tasteless and Keats was persuaded to remove a particularly brutal satirical description of the wedding guests. It is as if he is determined to demonstrate his new maturity of vision, his 'Judgement', by showing how far he can dissociate himself from the sentimentality and sensationalism of his subject-matter. But the reader may feel the strain of trying to see the poem with a kind of double vision, and there is no doubt that generations of critics have complained that 'Lamia' suffers from the lack of a clear, consistent point of view.

'Hyperion' and 'The Fall of Hyperion'

('Hyperion' was written between autumn 1818 and spring 1819, and published in *Poems*, 1820, subtitled 'A Fragment'. 'The Fall of Hyperion' was begun in July 1819 and abandoned in the autumn; it was not published in Keats's lifetime.)

Before Keats had even finished his Poetic Romance, 'Endymion', in November 1817 he was already making plans for an epic poem on a Classical theme. In January 1818 a letter to Haydon shows how far his thoughts had developed:

> in Endymion I think you may have many bits of the deep and sentimental cast—the nature of *Hyperion* will lead me to treat it in a more naked and grecian Manner—and the march of passion and endeavour will be undeviating—and one great contrast between them will be—that the Hero of the written tale ['Endymion'] being mortal is led on, like Buonaparte, by circumstance; whereas the Apollo in Hyperion being a fore-seeing God will shape his actions like one.

Keats also referred to the project in his Preface to 'Endymion' (published in May 1818). After apologising for the many signs of 'immaturity' and 'great inexperience' in the poem he concluded, 'I hope I have not in too late a day touched the beautiful mythology of Greece and dulled its brightness: for I wish to try once more, before I bid it farewell.'

Keats did not begin detailed work on 'Hyperion' until he returned from his summer tour of Scotland in 1818. Much of it was written in the intervals of nursing his brother, Tom, who died of tuberculosis at the beginning of December, and work on the poem was often a welcome escape from this unhappy occupation. 'This morning Poetry has conquered', Keats wrote to Reynolds in September, 'I have relapsed into those abstractions which are my only life.' From this period also date some of Keats's most famous remarks about the impersonality, the selflessness, of great artists and the ability of the 'camelion Poet' to enter 'the dark side of things' as well as the bright one. The trend of Keats's thinking was clearly above and beyond the merely personal, or was certainly struggling to be so. The word 'abstract' appears frequently in his correspondence; in October he wrote to George and Georgiana, 'The mighty abstract Idea I have of Beauty in all things stifles the more divided and minute domestic happiness— .... No sooner am I alone than shapes of epic greatness are stationed around me.' The unfinished epic, 'Hyperion', consists of only two Books, each of less than 400 lines, and a hundred or so lines of a third, but so far as it is possible to judge, it appears to be an attempt to demonstrate the invincible power of Beauty as a force in the process of evolution. Keats was a devout admirer of John Milton (1608–74) and 'Hyperion' contains many echoes of *Paradise Lost* in subject-matter and style. But, while Milton set out to 'justify the ways of God to men', Keats appears to have been trying to solve the problem of suffering by showing that 'first in beauty should be first in might'.

In the limited space of these Notes it is not possible to treat the 'Hyperion' fragments as fully as the poems already discussed. What follows, therefore, is, firstly a summary of 'Hyperion' with brief comments on its theme and style illustrated by quotations, and secondly a similar treatment of 'The Fall of Hyperion' with particular emphasis on Keats's changed approach in the second version of the poem.

'Hyperion'

The poem is based on the ancient Greek myth of the defeat of the old order of gods, the Titans, by their children, who then established themselves as the gods of Olympus. Keats was chiefly concerned with the replacement of the Titan sun-god, Hyperion, by the Olympian Apollo, god of the sun, healing, prophecy, music and poetry. In subject-matter and style Keats owed much to Milton and also to Dante (1265–1321). Dante's *Divina Commedia* ('Divine Comedy', a three-part description of a journey through Hell, Purgatory and Paradise) had been published in a new English translation by Henry Cary in 1814.

Book I opens with a description of Saturn, aged leader of the vanquished Titans, mourning his defeat in solitude, 'Deep in the shady sadness of a vale'. Eventually he is discovered by Thea, wife of Hyperion, who attempts to console him and the two grieve together, motionless, 'Like natural sculpture in cathedral cavern'. Hyperion, the only undefeated Titan, still reigns from his resplendent palace, 'Bastion'd with pyramids of glowing gold', but even he senses impending disaster and 'horrors, portion'd to a giant nerve,/Oft made Hyperion ache'. As he waits, impatient to burst out through the gates of dawn, he hears the voice of his father, Coelus, ancient god of the heavens, lamenting the war between his descendants. The gods have allowed themselves to act like mere mortals, governed by 'fear, hope and wrath ... rage and passion' and this has caused their fall. The Book ends as Hyperion sets out on his descent to find his defeated fellow-Titans.

The assembly of vanquished Titans at the beginning of Book II resembles the council of fallen angels in the second book of Milton's *Paradise Lost*, but Keats's victims are more sorrowful than angry. Saturn joins them and shares in their despair, but Oceanus, god of the seas, is more philosophical; he urges the Titans to accept their fate because, he claims, 'We fall by course of Nature's law.' Just as the Titans were superior to the chaos and darkness that preceded them, 'So on our heels a fresh perfection treads,/A power more strong in beauty, born of us/And fated to excel us.' Oceanus sums up the inevitable process: 'for 'tis the eternal law/That first in beauty should be first in might'. This strange evolutionary principle of the supremacy of beauty is an expression of Keats's belief that in both individual and social terms mankind obeys a law of progress. Although no easy optimist, Keats believed that a man might make his own soul by responding with heart and mind to the sufferings inflicted by the world, and that 'countries become gradually more enlighten'd'.

The Titans listened in silence to Oceanus's theory but eventually the goddess, Clymene, told them that she had heard the sounds of exquisite music from an island off the shore and a voice calling 'Apollo'. Enceladus next tried to rouse the Titans to action and greeted the approaching Hyperion.

The opening of Book III marks a noticeable change in style from the sonorous, measured cadences of Books I and II, with their many extended similes (see, for example, Book I, lines 72–8, 'As when, upon a tranced summer-night ... '). While still in blank verse, the lines move in more rapid, lilting rhythms and the poet begs his Muse to

Flush every thing that hath a vermeil hue,
Let the rose glow intense and warm the air,
And let the clouds of even and of morn
Float in voluptuous fleeces o'er the hills.

This soft, blushing, pulsating landscape, reminiscent of 'Endymion', proves to be the setting for Apollo, who, not yet a god, suffers in the midst of so much beauty from a mysterious sorrow. A goddess approaches him, whom he recognises as Mnemosyne, mother of the nine Muses and goddess of the arts, who first gave him his lyre. He asks her why he is so sad, and as he looks into her silent face he reads the story of all human suffering and 'Creations and destroyings, all at once /Pour into the wide hollows of my brain'. This insight transforms Apollo into a god and, in agony akin to a death-throe, he is reborn as a divine creature. Here, in mid-sentence, the narrative breaks off.

There is no need to look further for a reason for Keats's abandonment of work on 'Hyperion' than the death of Tom at the beginning of December; he made several attempts to continue the poem but, not surprisingly, confessed that 'I have not been in great cue for writing lately' (February 1819). His contemporaries regarded the first two Books of 'Hyperion' as Keats's finest achievement, for sustained grandeur of vision and style, for their clarity of structure, and for the promise of heroic action on a truly epic scale. Tastes have changed and nowadays the odes of 1819 are more widely admired, but the completed Books of 'Hyperion' are still considered a magnificent technical achievement, Miltonic in tone and style and yet modified (as F.R. Leavis has pointed out in *Revaluation*) by Keats's characteristic taste for 'Spenserian vowels that elope with ease'. There is also general agreement that the fragment of Book III with its 'pillowy', scented softness and concentration on Apollo's personal pain represents a lapse from the impersonal, tragic drama of Books I and II.

'The Fall of Hyperion'

When in Book III of 'Hyperion' Apollo reads the history of human suffering in Mnemosyne's face, he cries 'Knowledge enormous makes a God of me'. It is this process, the transformation of a human poet into a godlike being through the knowledge of suffering, that preoccupied Keats when he returned to the Hyperion theme in July 1819. But now the poet in question was not the fictional character, Apollo, but the poet-narrator himself. 'The Fall of Hyperion', subtitled 'A Dream', consists of only one Canto of 467 lines, and 60 or so lines of a second. (A 'canto', from the Italian for 'song' or 'melody', means a section of a long poem that could be recited or 'sung' by a minstrel without a break. Keats's use of the term shows the influence of Dante, whose *Divina Commedia* is divided into cantos.) Most of the first Canto of 'The Fall of Hyperion' consists of a prologue to the main narrative in which Keats presents himself as poet-narrator coming face to face with Moneta (a priestess, daughter of Mnemosyne) and learning from her what it is to understand suffering, and to be a true poet.

Canto I opens with a brief reflection on the human tendency to dream and to have visions, and leaves posterity to judge the validity of what follows. Using the convention, common in medieval poetry, of the 'dream-vision', the poet describes how he discovered in a forest the abandoned remains of a lavish banquet; having eaten and drunk some of the delicious food and wine he fell into a deep sleep. When he awoke he found himself in an enormous, ancient temple, at the end of which he could see a mysterious figure sitting at the top of a flight of steps, high above an altar. As he approached a voice warned him that if he could not climb the steps he would die where he stood, on the cold marble floor. Desperately fighting the paralysing effect of the icy cold, the poet managed to mount the stairs and, confronting the veiled figure, asked why he alone should be saved from death.

In the dialogue that follows the figure explained that the poet had been spared because he had been willing to risk death before its appointed time. Only those who were sensitive to human suffering could reach the top of the steps, the selfish and insensitive died on the floor below, while those who had lovingly served their fellow-men never needed to enter this temple. The figure accused the poet of being 'a dreaming thing' who 'venoms all his days,/Bearing more woe than all his sins deserve'. The poet tried to justify his art, claiming that 'a poet is a sage;/A humanist, physician to all men' but the figure replied that he was a dreamer, not a true poet. While the poet 'pours out a balm upon the world' the dreamer 'vexes it'. At this the poet cried out in despair to Apollo to help him and to tell him who this mysterious figure was.

Then the figure explained sadly that she was Moneta, the only priestess to survive the downfall of Saturn, and offered to reveal to the mortal eyes of the poet all the pain she knew and suffered. Drawing aside her veil she revealed a face of unearthly pallor and 'blank' but 'benignant' eyes. The poet begged her to show him what caused her expression of mourning:

I ached to see what things the hollow brain
Behind enwombed: what high tragedy
In the dark secret chambers of her skull
Was acting...

No sooner had the poet uttered this request than he and Moneta found themselves transported to a spot 'Deep in the shady sadness of a vale', and from this point the narrative picks up the account of the defeated Saturn from the opening of 'Hyperion', Book I, but with the addition of Moneta and the poet as spectators and with the inclusion of the poet's own reactions. As he watched the mourning Saturn, the poet felt 'A power within me of enormous ken,/To see as a God sees'. As

Saturn voiced his rage and despair to Thea the poet commented, 'Methought I heard some old man of the earth/Bewailing earthly loss', and struggled to reconcile the noble appearance of Saturn with the wildness of his words.

Canto II opens with Moneta's description of the palace of Hyperion, and then, as she and the poet witness the arrival of the sun-god in all his splendour, the narrative breaks off.

Keats gave his reasons for abandoning 'The Fall of Hyperion' in a letter to J.H. Reynolds on 21 September 1819:

> I have given up Hyperion—there were too many Miltonic inversions in it—Miltonic verse cannot be written but in an artful or rather artist's humour. I wish to give myself up to other sensations. English ought to be kept up. It may be interesting to you to pick out some lines from Hyperion and put a mark X to the false beauty proceeding from art, and one II to the true voice of feeling.

This explanation concentrates on matters of style, but in changing the opening of the poem as he had done Keats had also given himself considerable difficulties of structure and content. What was the central subject of the new poem to be? The tragic fate of Hyperion? Or the consciousness of the poet as he shares in, but is not destroyed by, the tragic events he is allowed to witness? The dialogue with Moneta had contained some of the most penetrating questions about the poet's function and the value of art in relation to life. How was the tragedy of the Titans, a race of legendary, superhuman beings, to benefit 'poor humanity' or contribute to 'mortal good'? The many religious images and symbols of Canto I demonstrate how seriously Keats regarded the attainment of a true vision of human tragedy. The poet's willingness to die in order to achieve a life of greater understanding is an idea shared by the religious of many faiths. Keats himself was not religious in any orthodox sense; he might be described as a secular humanist with a strong, intuitive belief in some form of personal immortality. But the desire to attain insight is urgently repeated:

> To see as a God sees, and take the depth
> Of things as nimbly as the outward eye
> Can size and shape pervade . . .

This kind of poetic self-consciousness can, however, degenerate into the most narcissistic form of art, and in 'The Fall of Hyperion' Keats may have found himself drifting into that most introverted form of poetry whose sole subject is the poet's uncertainty about his own role. In 'Sleep and Poetry' (1816) he had promised to aim for 'a nobler life, /Where I may find the agonies, the strife/Of human hearts'; 'The Fall of Hyperion' was the final stage in that uncompleted search.

Part 3

Commentary

John Keats and 'Johnny Keats'

'Johnny Keats' was the nickname, said to have been invented by Lord Byron, used by reviewers hostile to Leigh Hunt and his associates, the so-called 'Cockney School of Poetry'. The diminutive form was intended as a slighting reference to Keats's lower-middle-class background and to what was considered the vulgarity of his poetic style. Nowadays we regard the attack as vulgar as well as unjustified, but there has always been a sense in which critics, however sympathetic to Keats and his work, have been embarrassed by an awkward division in his poetry between the sensuous and the serious. There is the thinking John Keats, so to speak, and 'Johnny Keats', the lover of mere sensation. One recent literary historian has called Keats 'the most sensual of English poets'* and the Victorian critic, Matthew Arnold (1822–88), claimed that 'No one can question the eminency, in Keats's poetry, of the quality of sensuousness.' He was also quick to point out emphatically, however, that 'Keats had flint and iron in him.' Keats himself was well aware of the contrary impulses in his own nature; in the spring of 1818, when he was planning a programme of travel and self-education, he wrote to his publisher, 'I have been hovering for some time between an exquisite sense of the luxurious and a love for Philosophy.'

Keats believed in evolution, in the possibility of social and personal improvement, and in his own potential for development as a man and a poet. In your review of Keats's work as a whole you might find it helpful to consider, on the basis of the letters as well as the poems, how far 'Johnny' was displaced by the maturer John Keats. You should look at some of the poems in the 1817 collection (such as 'I stood tip-toe upon a little hill', 'To Charles Cowden Clarke' and 'Sleep and Poetry'), and at least one book of 'Endymion' as well as the contents of *Poems*, 1820 (most of which have been discussed in detail in Part 2 of these Notes). Critical discussion tends to concentrate on the conflicts, tensions and developments in Keats's art, so you may find the following lists helpful. Ask yourself how far Keats succeeds in resolving these pairs of opposed ideas or qualities:

* G.S. Fraser, in *A Short History of English Poetry*, Open Books, Shepton Mallet, 1981, p.219.

sensation	– thought	imagination	– truth
pleasure	– pain	'poesy'	– poetry
illusion	– reality	possession	– loss
ideal	– actual	eternal	– mortal
self	– the world	art	– life
	dreaming	– normal consciousness	
	feeling (how I feel)	– feel (this is how it feels)	

In your thinking keep a clear sense of the chronology of the events of Keats's life and the sequence of his ideas as well as the order of his poems, in particular the extraordinarily fruitful year from the autumn of 1818 ('Hyperion'), through early 1819 ('The Eve of St Agnes', 'La Belle Dame sans Merci' and the Spring odes) to the late summer and autumn ('Lamia', 'The Fall of Hyperion' and 'To Autumn').

'O for a life of Sensations rather than of Thoughts!'

(Letter to Benjamin Bailey, 22 November 1817)
This exclamation, taken out of context, is often used as evidence to support the argument that Keats was a mindless hedonist. But the same letter contains a declaration of faith in 'the holiness of the Heart's affections and the truth of Imagination' as well as a discussion of the lack of egocentricity characteristic of men of true genius, the quality he was to define a few weeks later as 'Negative Capability, that is when man is capable of being in uncertainties, Mysteries, doubts, without any irritable reaching after fact & reason' (Letter to George and Tom Keats, 21, 27? December 1817). The issue here is the question of an intuitive rather than a rational approach to knowledge, and not a mere hunger for sensual gratification. Yet there is no doubt that Keats's responsiveness to sense-experience is the source of his greatest strength as well as his most pronounced weaknesses as a poet; his ability to render the precise quality of actual sensation in images of surprising originality and reassuring exactness is a rare talent that all his admirers recognise.

On the other hand, when Keats allows his imagination to ramble in fantasy, particularly in the realm of erotic wish-fulfilment, the effect can be mere word-spinning or absurdity, as, for example, in 'Endymion', where kisses are described as 'slippery blisses' and 'nectarous camel-draughts'. And in 'The Fall of Hyperion', when the allegorical action reaches a pitch of intensity as the poet struggles for his life, we are confronted with the bathos of

One minute before death, my iced foot touch'd
The lowest stair; and as it touch'd, life seem'd
To pour in at the toes.

One image from Shakespeare's erotic poem, *Venus and Adonis*, particularly impressed Keats: '...as the snail, whose tender horns being hit,/Shrinks backwards in his shelly cave with pain.' This image is an appropriate metaphor for Keats's own sensitive faculty of perception; he once said in the Lake District, 'I live in the eye; and my imagination, surpassed, is at rest' (letter to Tom Keats, 22–7 June 1818). His visual images, with their emotive details of colour and light, are memorably rich and vivid. But Keats has also been called 'the poet of touch-and-taste' and it is noticeable how often food and drink, and the actual sensations of eating and drinking, figure in his poetry. Remember the banquets of 'Lamia' and 'The Fall of Hyperion', the array of exotic delicacies in 'The Eve of St Agnes' and the references to food and wine in the Spring odes, and consider their closeness of association with sexuality and with a kind of spiritual hunger as well as with normal, physical appetite. Keats considered that 'A Man's life of any worth is a continual allegory' (letter to George and Georgiana Keats, February to May 1819), and these elaborately detailed feasts are charged with a more than literal significance.

We think of the typical Romantic artist as a lonely figure, separated from the world by his wish and ability to see beyond it, but at the same time longing for union with it, a sense of 'oneness' with the whole of nature. This gulf may be bridged by making the world a part of oneself, by literally consuming it as food, or by regarding it, as Keats so often does, as nourishment for the soul. Union with another person in the act of sexual love is another way of losing one's sense of 'otherness'; notice the possibility of a double meaning of 'solution' in these lines from 'The Eve of St Agnes':

Into her dream he melted, as the rose
Blendeth its odour with the violet,—
Solution sweet.

'Solution' means, literally, 'fusion' or 'mixture', but an overtone of 'resolution', as of a problem solved, is also possible. Yet this moment of union and intense delight is the most fleeting of all pleasures, and sexual ecstasy in Keats's poetry is the chief instance of 'aching Pleasure' that turns into the pain of loss even as it is experienced.

When Keats combines associations with all five senses he often achieves a concentrated richness of effect which suggests the comprehensiveness of actual, felt experience. Remember, for example, the density of stanzas 2 and 5 of the 'Ode to a Nightingale': 'O for a beaker full of the warm South' and 'I cannot see...what soft incense hangs upon the boughs.' (The latter image recalls the startling physicality of Shakespeare's, 'From the barge/A strange invisible perfume hits the sense/Of the adjacent wharfs', *Antony and Cleopatra*, Act II, Scene

2.) But, even here, notice that it would be wrong to describe the experience as purely physical: taste stimulates memory, a nostalgia for the pastoral landscape of classical mythology. And as one association sets off another, the poet recalls the properties of wine, to inspire creativity or to drug into unconsciousness. Remember, too, the imagery of the Chapman's Homer sonnet, where one kind of excitement, the intellectual and emotional excitement over the discovery of a new text, is dramatised as a much more physical reaction to the unexpected vastness of a new ocean.

'A very gradual ripening of the intellectual powers'

(Letter to George and Tom Keats, 23, 24 January 1818)
Not many talented, idealistic and ambitious twenty-two year-olds are as patient as Keats, who recognised that 'great productions' emerge only after a long, slow process of intellectual growth. Notice his metaphorical use of 'ripening', and remember that in 'To Autumn' the final stages of ripening and harvesting move at a pace hardly perceptible to the human eye: 'with patient look,/Thou watchest the last oozings hours by hours'. Keats wrote to Reynolds in May 1818, 'An extensive knowledge is needful to thinking people—it takes away the heat and fever; and helps, by widening speculation, to ease the Burden of the Mystery.' Later on in the same letter Keats developed what he called 'a simile of human life', and it is worth quoting at length because it shows not only his capacity for detached, objective thought, but also his habit of thinking in concrete, physical terms:

> I compare human life to a large Mansion of Many Apartments...
> The first we step into we call the infant or thoughtless Chamber, in which we remain as long as we do not think—We remain there a long while, and notwithstanding the doors of the second Chamber remain wide open, showing a bright appearance, we care not to hasten to it; but are at length imperceptibly impelled by the awakening of the thinking principle ... We no sooner get into the second Chamber, which I shall call the Chamber of Maiden-Thought, than we become intoxicated with the light and the atmosphere ... and think of delaying there for ever in delight: However among the effects this breathing is father of is that tremendous one of sharpening one's vision into the heart and nature of Man—of convincing ones nerves that the World is full of Misery and Heartbreak, Pain, Sickness and oppression—whereby This Chamber of Maiden Thought becomes gradually darken'd and at the same time on all sides of it many doors are set open—but all dark—all leading to dark passages—we see not the ballance of good and evil. We are in a Mist —*We* are now in that state—We feel the 'burden of the Mystery'.

The thought is presented as a nightmarish vision; notice that Keats talks of convincing, not one's mind, but one's *nerves* of the condition of the world. To Keats ideas and human truths could not simply be intellectually apprehended, they had to be fully experienced to be accepted. Elsewhere in the letter quoted above he had written, 'axioms in philosophy are not axioms until they are proved upon our pulses'. Our pulse-rate is a bodily function over which we have no conscious control unless we are trained in a discipline such as yoga; it races when we are excited or frightened and slows when we are ill. So Keats is claiming that a truth is not valid unless it accords with our instincts and intuitions. Widely applied, this idea could be dangerous; a violent and brutal person could interpret it as a licence for all kinds of destructive behaviour. Blushing is one of those physical reactions over which we have no control: it is a proof of something on 'our pulses', but it is also a moral response to circumstances. We blush for guilt, shame or embarrassment when we are instinctively conscious that something is wrong. In his book, *Keats and Embarrassment* (Oxford University Press, 1974), Christopher Ricks has shown from the many references to blushing in Keats's poems and letters that he was a person in whom this instinctive moral sense was very highly developed. This combination of moral and physical hypersensitivity appears in some of the extreme reactions to circumstances in the poems, such as Porphyro's 'faintness' as he watches Madeline at prayer in 'The Eve of St Agnes': 'She knelt, so pure a thing, so free from mortal taint.' Porphyro's perfectly natural desire to make love to Madeline conflicts with the knowledge that in so doing he will violate her chastity.

Although Keats set a high value on knowledge and thought and accepted the necessity of suffering as part of the progress to moral and spiritual maturity, he was not an abstract thinker and greatly disliked art that was overtly didactic. 'We hate poetry that has a palpable design upon us', he wrote to Reynolds in January 1818. But his own work did become more morally ambitious; notice that in his early poems he delighted in Classical myth for its own sake ('the realm of Flora and old Pan'), whereas later he adapted it to function symbolically in his vision of the human drama. In 'Hyperion', Saturn, Hyperion and Apollo are not just figures from ancient legend, they are representatives of an old and a new order of society. And consider Keats's choice of a *Greek* urn in the ode in which he wrestles with the paradoxical relationship of life and art. Why would a modern statue or a vase with a non-figurative design not have suited his purpose just as well? When Keats is categoric and didactic, as, for example, in the last lines of the 'Ode on a Grecian Urn', we feel the effect to be forced, strained and uncharacteristic. His natural mode is questioning and particular rather than assertive and general. The odes (with the exception of 'To Autumn') are dramatic presentations of the poet's own uncertainties and conflicts, and it is these that carry conviction rather than the somewhat forced and facile equation of 'Beauty and Truth'. Keats was born into a debate about the relationship between these two concepts that had originated far back in the eighteenth century, and his wholehearted commitment to 'the Principle of Beauty' was often in conflict with his practical realism, rooted in the experience of everyday life and human behaviour. In this, Keats was most unlike Shelley, for whom abstractions had a genuine reality. Had the term 'Romanticism' even existed in Keats's lifetime (which of course it did not), it is unlikely that he would have had much patience with it. There are those who consider that Keats, in spite of his passion for 'the beautiful', is the least typical of the so-called Romantic poets; his realism, although less developed in his poems than in his letters, sets him apart from the literary and artistic fashions of his time.

'Misers of sound and syllable let us be'*

From 'Hyperion' onwards Keats was working for a denser, more concentrated effect in his poetry. In August 1820 he presumed to give the following advice to Shelley: 'You might curb your magnanimity and be more of an artist, and "load every rift" of your subject with ore.' (The phrase Keats quotes is from Spenser's *Faerie Queene*.) G.S. Fraser has noticed how Keats 'fingers words for the right combination of concentrated sensuous expressiveness and musical surprise'. Detailed studies have shown how Keats gradually abandoned the adjectives with a '-y' ending (such as 'milky', 'rosy', 'bloomy') characteristic of his early verse, and substituted the much more vigorous past participle of the verb, as 'Tall oaks, branch-*charmed* by the earnest stars', 'her *warmed* jewels', '*unravish'd* bride of quietness', thus investing the descriptions with the energy of the active verb. This shift in style has often been described as a movement from 'feminine' to 'masculine' and is a favourite topic for examiners even though nowadays we may find the implications offensive.

Keats left no detailed, written theory of metrics, but we know from his friend Bailey that he was particularly interested in 'the principle of Melody in verse' and especially 'the management of open & close vowels'. These were probably what we would call 'long' and 'short' vowels, as, for example, long vowels in 'pain', 'stain', 'stone' and short vowels in 'fan', 'sin', 'sun'. Keats believed that 'the vowels should be so managed as not to clash one with another so as to mar the melody,—& yet that they should be interchanged, like differing notes

---

* Sonnet, 'If by dull rhymes our English must be chain'd'.

of music to prevent monotony'. We might describe this as a theory of assonance rather than a strictly 'melodic' effect, but notice what a powerful rhythmical pattern is established when the metrical stress falls on long syllables that also echo each other in sound, as in these lines from stanza 24 of 'The Eve of St Agnes':

> And díamonded with pánes of quáint devíce,
> Innumerable of stáins and splendid dýes,
> As are the tíger-moth's deep-damask'd wings . . .

In this example only the stressed syllables that make up the pattern of assonance are marked; as the lines are in iambic pentameter there are in fact five strong stresses in each line. 'The Eve of St Agnes' is particularly rich in these melodic effects, and it is fascinating to see how different the impression of the verse can be in a stanza where Keats has used a much higher proportion of short vowels:

> And still she slept an azure-lidded sléep,   (1)
>
> In blánched linen, smóoth and lavender'd . . .   (2)
>
> With jellies sóother than the créamy cúrd,   (3)
>
> And Lúcent syrops, tinct with cinnamon   (1)

The figure in brackets at the end of the line refers to the total number of long vowels in that line, and only the long vowels have been given their stress-marks. How much more rapidly and lightly these lines move than those quoted above from stanza 24.

Some people are reluctant to look at poetry in this kind of technical light, and find metrical analysis mechanical and boring. However, you should remember that Keats and his contemporaries took the craft of poetry very seriously; Keats knew that much of 'Endymion' was 'slip-shod', with forced rhymes, awkward rhythms and clumsy phrases. We are neglecting a great part of Keats's achievement if we are unappreciative of his quality as a lyric poet. It is very difficult to discuss the musical quality of poetry on the printed page, so try, preferably with a friend, to read the poems aloud, not hurrying or skipping words, listening for the rhyme-words and the natural fall of the emphasis. Remember that poets are people who enjoy words, enjoy playing with them, and exploit every possible aspect of them: their sense, their sounds, their 'atmospheres' (Keats particularly liked the word 'vale' because it seemed to him to have a cool sound). You might begin with the ballad, 'Old Meg she was a gipsey', written during Keats's tour of Scotland, in which the emphatic rhythm and rhyme almost overwhelm the sense, and then go for contrast to the much more subtle and sophisticated pattern of one of the 1819 odes. Remember that you will normally need to pronounce the '-ed' ending of the past participle of the verb for the line to scan correctly; the edition of the poems used in these Notes substitutes an apostrophe when the final syllable is not pronounced, for example, 'unravish'd', 'leaf-fring'd'. If your edition does not make this distinction, you will have to judge very carefully whether the '-ed' endings are to be pronounced or not.

Keats attracted a great deal of hostile criticism in his lifetime for his unorthodox imagery and experimental use of language. But while in some respects an innovator he was in many ways a conservative in his approach to verse forms. Many conventional forms were available to him: the different forms of the sonnet, blank verse, the ode, the heroic couplet, the Spenserian stanza, the ballad. Keats saw no need to break with tradition; on the contrary, he aimed to achieve mastery of the forms in which Spenser, Shakespeare, Milton and Wordsworth had excelled. He had immense technical facility as a poet; he and his friends used to have poetry competitions, 'sonnet-races' to see who could write the best sonnet in a quarter of an hour. Keats's 'On the Grasshopper and the Cricket' is said to be the result of such a competition with Leigh Hunt. (Try to write a technically correct Shakespearean or Petrarchan sonnet yourself and see how long it takes you, to get an idea of Keats's command of form. You will find it is less difficult than you expect.) But perhaps one of the most inhibiting pressures that Keats suffered was the sense of obligation to prove his seriousness as a poet by completing a long poem. 'Endymion' was the result of this compulsion to produce four thousand lines of verse, and throughout his working life he was impelled towards the epic as the 'noblest' form of poetry, and the truest test of his standing as a poet. This is perhaps not surprising in an age when prose fiction was only just establishing itself as a form of literature to be taken seriously, both morally and aesthetically. In 1820 the great novelists of the eighteenth century, Henry Fielding (1707–54) and Samuel Richardson (1689–1761) were long dead, Jane Austen (born 1775) had died three years previously, and Sir Walter Scott (1771–1832) had published only a fraction of his enormous output of novels. Charles Dickens (1812–70) and the Brontës (Charlotte 1816–55, Emily 1818–48) were still only children, George Eliot (1819–80) was a baby and Thomas Hardy, Henry James and Joseph Conrad still unborn. In Keats's day the long poem was the vehicle for fiction of a serious, philosophic nature in an elevated style. It is ironic that Keats is now most widely celebrated for poems that he considered almost peripheral; for Keats, even 'Lamia' was only a 'short' poem.

Part 4

Hints for study

IF YOU HAVE FOLLOWED these Notes carefully and worked through the poems in the order given in Part 2, you should have acquired a good working knowledge of a representative sample of Keats's major poetry. However, if you have not yet done this you should turn back to the beginning of Part 2 and work through it slowly before attempting to use this section. What follows is not an instant, foolproof recipe for success in an examination, and if you try to tackle this section before you have got to know the poems well for yourself, you will not find it helpful. You cannot develop your own ideas with confidence without a thorough, detailed knowledge of the text; when you have achieved this you will find the exercises that follow easy and straightforward.

Collecting material and sorting out ideas

Read through the poems discussed in Part 2 again, keeping to their chronological order, and make notes when you find examples under the following headings:

(i) *Themes and ideas*
>   —transience: the short-lived nature of beauty and happiness
>   —pleasure and pain: the relationship between them and the value of suffering
>   —the value of enduring art and the role of the poet
>   —myth and the supernatural
>   —Keats's attitude to women; Keats as a love-poet

(ii) *Forms and styles*
>   —narrative poems; Keats's skill as a storyteller in handling events and characters
>   —dramatic qualities in the poems
>   —Keats as a sonneteer and the evolution of the odes from the sonnet form

(iii) *Diction and imagery*
>   —'feminine' and 'masculine'
>   —the five senses; synaesthesia; colour
>   —melody; Keats as a lyric poet

You may wish to add other headings of your own; you will certainly discover more as you go along. You will probably find it helpful to use a separate sheet of paper for each set of notes; this will keep each individual category clear, and will give you space to jot down your own ideas as you go along. If you store the pages in a loose-leaf file with coloured dividing cards you will find it very easy to trace references when you want them for essays or revision.

Selecting quotations to illustrate arguments

As you make notes on the points listed above, you will probably come across lines and phrases in the poems that illustrate vividly and concisely a recurrent theme or a characteristic response to experience. Make notes of these as you discover them, under the headings suggested above. For example, under 'the five senses' you might very well include stanza 2 of the 'Ode to a Nightingale' and under 'colour' stanza 24 of 'The Eve of St Agnes'. Eventually you will need to select a number of these quotations to learn by heart so that you can back up your argument with Keats's own words in an examination; no examiner will give you much credit for your ideas unless you can show that you have precise, detailed evidence for them. Some people find it easier to remember a selection of single lines and short phrases, but many more would find it very rewarding to memorise a number of complete poems from which to select illustrations for a wide variety of topics. Poems chosen would be the ode 'To Autumn' and either 'Ode to a Nightingale' or 'Ode on a Grecian Urn', the sonnet on Chapman's Homer and two or three stanzas from 'The Eve of St Agnes' (you might like to guess *which* stanzas). If this choice seems to you rather hackneyed and obvious, you will certainly get a great deal of satisfaction from making your own selection, but try to ensure that you collect a good 'all-purpose' range, for none of us has a perfect memory and it is better to have a short list that can be quoted accurately than a long list that becomes blurred and inaccurate in the stress of the examination room.

You will need to be able to quote from Keats's letters as well as from his poems. No one will expect you to be able to reproduce long extracts word-for-word, but you should be able to refer closely to passages where Keats discusses some of his main preoccupations, such as:
—beauty and truth
—'negative capability' and the chameleon poet
—the truth of imagination
—man's life a mansion of many chambers
—the world as 'a vale of soul-making'
—'intensity' and 'gusto' the qualities of great art
—experience as the test of knowledge

The key here is to study each idea or phrase in its particular context. 'Negative capability', for example, is in isolation a peculiar concept, but in the context of a letter in which Keats is discussing Shakespeare's *King Lear*, Coleridge and a picture called 'Death on a Pale Horse', the idea is very much more comprehensible (letter to George and Tom Keats, December 1817).

Extending your reading

If English is *not* your first language, you may feel you have more than enough to do in mastering the poems discussed in these Notes and getting to know a selection from the letters. But if English *is* your first language, you should not limit yourself to the poems discussed in Part 2; be adventurous and read more widely in both Keats's poems and letters. Examiners always give credit for signs of independent work as opposed to mere 'parrot-repetition'. If you are interested in Keats's development as a poet, look at more of the early poetry; if you want to discuss his skill in narrative you should read 'Isabella' and at least part of 'Endymion'; if you are preparing for a question on Keats's dramatic ambitions and abilities, you must pay some attention to 'Otho the Great'. And always bear in mind that time spent getting to know the poems and developing your own ideas about them is ten times more valuable than any critical or background reading. If you want to know more about Romanticism, read the works of Wordsworth, Coleridge, Shelley and Byron and draw your own conclusions; such first-hand insights are far more valuable and exciting than lists of names and dates in a reference book. Remember that Keats got his inspiration from reading Homer, Spenser, Shakespeare and Milton for himself, not by reading books *about* them, and follow his example.

Some essay topics

(1) Do you agree that the Odes demonstrate 'the painful antithesis between transient sensation and enduring art'?

Be wary of jumping to the conclusion that this question expects an unqualified 'yes' for an answer. The 'Ode on a Grecian Urn' certainly presents the conflict between fleeting sensation and the permanence of art, but is this equally true of the 'Ode to a Nightingale' where the song is the natural voice of a wild creature and therefore not strictly speaking a work of art, although it is beautiful? And does the question of art enter into the 'Ode on Melancholy'? There is pain, certainly, at 'Beauty that must die', but no reference to a work of art. And what about the 'Ode to Psyche', where there is no conflict though the poet triumphs in the power of his imagination to create something of lasting beauty? 'To Autumn', the least painful of the odes, is a celebration of the ripeness of nature and a serene acceptance of transience as part of the natural cycle.

(2) 'The poetry of earth is never dead.' Consider the poetry of Keats (with some reference to his letters) as a celebration of the world of natural objects.

This is almost the opposite of question (1); you might begin with 'To Autumn' as an example of such a celebration, and cite the sonnet 'On the Sea' and passages from 'The Eve of St Agnes' as further instances of Keats's delight in the natural world. Passages from the letters on the Lake District and the mountains of Scotland could also be referred to. But you might conclude that Keats was also aware of the limitations of the mortal world, the inevitability of decay and death, and looked to the world of the imagination to provide imperishable examples of beauty. This is the particular power and value of the urn, symbolising the permanence of art.

(3) Keats's greatest ambition was 'the writing of a few fine plays'. What evidence do you find of dramatic powers in his poetry?

Bear in mind that the essence of drama is character in action, so you must consider where in his poems Keats most successfully presents individual human beings reacting to circumstances and to each other. You might decide that the narrative poems contain some dramatic elements—the dialogues between Lamia and Lycius, for example, and Porphyro's encounters with Angela and Madeline. But you might feel that 'Hyperion' is too static, its characters too statuesque, to qualify as drama. And you might feel that the poems which contain most drama are those in which the central character is the poet himself, as he grapples with intense and painful feeling in the odes of the spring of 1819 and in Canto I of 'The Fall of Hyperion'.

(4) How far do you find the same personality in Keats's letters and poems?

This is a fascinating topic for anyone who knows the letters well, offering a chance to refer to Keats's robust sense of humour (not often seen in the poems), and his attractive social self as well as the maturer, humane insights that were only beginning to show themselves in the poetry when he died.

(5) 'The Cliff of Poesy towers above me.' Discuss the view that one of the major themes in the poems and letters of Keats is his concern with his mastery and understanding of the poetic art.

This is a good, straightforward topic; 'Sleep and Poetry' and 'The Fall of Hyperion' would be appropriate points to begin and end.

(6) By close reference to one good and one bad poem show what you consider to be Keats's greatest strengths and weaknesses as a poet.

Here is an opportunity for you to exercise your own critical judgement. Remember that, while it may be easy to sense whether something is good or bad, it is not always easy to express this feeling in words.

(7) Do you agree that Keats's poetry, at its best, strikes a perfect balance between the real and the visionary?

This is a tricky question; what does 'a perfect balance' mean? Keats often makes his visions seem real through his use of vivid, physical imagery, though the reader is sometimes left (as in the uncompleted Hyperion poems) wondering what the vision means. The odes probably provide the clearest examples of visionary experiences dramatised as something physically and emotionally lived through in the duration of the poem.

(8) How far do Keats's poems illustrate his ideas expressed in the letters on the value of suffering?

It could be argued that they do not do this very much. The Keats of the letters appears to have developed a tragic insight far in advance of anything expressed in the poems, even in the Hyperion poems, which clearly set out to face the problems of suffering and loss. In the poetry, human ills are referred to in very general terms ('The weariness, the fever and the fret'), whereas pleasurable sensations are treated much more specifically. However, it might also be argued on the evidence of the last few lines of the 'Ode on Melancholy', that intense happiness and sensitivity to pleasure are only available to those who have also experienced acute pain.

(9) Discuss the relationship between thoughts and sense-impressions in Keats's poetry.

For a discussion of sensation and thought, see Part 3 of these Notes.

(10) Write a critical analysis of 'The Fall of Hyperion', Canto I, lines 52–80, showing in what ways it is typical of Keats's poetry.

First of all, before you even look at the passage, think and make some notes about the qualities that would enable you to recognise a passage of poetry as by Keats and not by, say, Shakespeare, Milton, Shelley or a modern poet. Then turn to the passage and look carefully at its subject-matter, diction, imagery, rhythm and rhyme (if any). Consider its quality; is it typical of Keats at his best or his worst? Is it even typical of Keats at all? . . . Always read essay and examination questions very carefully.

(11) Discuss the range and variety of Keats's narrative technique.

The key word in this question is 'technique'; the question asks for a more analytical approach than a mere list of Keats's narrative poems. The narrative poems are a favourite topic with examiners, so a full essay is offered here.

In Keats's time the long, narrative poem was both popular and highly regarded as a literary form. Wordsworth's *The Excursion*, a long, philosophical poem in blank verse, was published in 1814, and Lord Byron was able to command large sums of money for his dashing tales of romantic adventures. Keats felt that he had to prove himself as a poet by producing a poem of substantial length and 'Endymion', his story, in four thousand lines, of a quest for ideal love, was his first, and unhappily unsuccessful, attempt to do so. But as a reader and a writer Keats loved poetry that tells a story. In his short working life 'the beautiful mythology of Greece', the heroic epics of Homer (in English translation), Edmund Spenser's allegorical, romantic epic, *The Faerie Queene*, and Milton's Christian epic, *Paradise Lost*, served as inspiration, source-material and stylistic models for Keats.

Keats's first known poem, a fragment only a few lines long, was a deliberate 'Imitation of Spenser' and in it he reproduced the enamelled brilliance of Spenser's diction and the complicated nine-line Spenserian stanza form (rhyming *a b a b b c b c c*). The Spenserian stanza was also the medium for what is perhaps Keats's most completely successful and self-consistent narrative poem, 'The Eve of St Agnes'. In this tale of the triumph of young love over adversity the action is set in the atmosphere of medieval romance, and the poem is rich in vivid, sensuous detail. Keats was somewhat self-critical of his abilities as a storyteller, however, and considered that he had subordinated his characters to scene-setting and 'drapery'. He had been even more critical of an earlier narrative poem, 'Isabella; or, The Pot of Basil', in which young love ended in tragedy; it was full of melodramatic incidents and grue-some details, and Keats thought it betrayed his ignorance and inexper-ience of human behaviour. It was written in the Italianate verse-form of ottava rima (an eight-line stanza, rhyming *a b a b a b c c*), an approp-riate choice, for the source of the story was the *Decameron*, a collec-tion of tales by the fourteenth-century Italian writer, Boccaccio.

Keats's versatility as a poet shows in his willingness to experiment with a variety of verse-forms. In 'Endymion' he used the rhyming couplet, but the strain of sustaining this through four thousand lines shows in many forced and awkward rhymes. But in 'Lamia', the last of Keats's narratives on the theme of love, he handled the couplet with much more ease and fluency, sometimes turning the rhyme to satirical effect, as in this aside to the reader:

> Love in a hut, with water and crust,
> Is—Love, forgive us!—cinders, ashes, dust;
> Love in a palace is perhaps at last
> More grievous torment than a hermit's fast—

Keats's admiration for Shakespeare and for Milton meant that when he returned to the world of Classical legend about a year after completing 'Endymion', determined to treat it 'in a more naked and Grecian manner', his choice of medium was blank verse. 'Hyperion' and 'The Fall of Hyperion' show a marked change in style and tone from the luxuriant word-spinning of 'Endymion' and the restrained eroticism of 'The Eve of St Agnes'. The tone is lofty and dignified, with long, con-trolled sentences and extended similes in the Miltonic idiom. Keats was now using Classical legend not as mere decoration, but as an allegory to illustrate his tragic theme.

Keats had a passionate admiration for Shakespeare and one of his greatest ambitions was to write 'a few fine plays'. He considered that the sign of a great artist was his ability to subordinate his own personal-ity to create entirely convincing fictional characters, such as the Shake-spearean heroes that the actor, Edmund Kean, performed with such 'gusto'. Keats's own forceful personality often appears in his narrat-ives in the voice of the narrator, interrupting and commenting upon events, almost as if he did not trust the story to speak for itself. However, in one short poem in which the story emerges in conversation through a process of question and answer, Keats reveals himself a master of narrative method. The ballad, 'La Belle Dame sans Merci', concentrates into its twelve short stanzas more suspense, pathos and mystery than Keats was able to suggest in many of his much longer and more ambitious poems.

Part 5

Suggestions for further reading

The poems

The text of Keats's own poems used in these Notes is *The Poems of John Keats*, edited by Jack Stillinger, Heinemann, London, 1978. Two fully annotated editions of the complete poems, *The Poems of John Keats*, edited by Miriam Allott, Longman, London, 1970 and *John Keats: The Complete Poems*, edited by John Barnard, Penguin Books, Harmondsworth, second edition, 1977, are also frequently referred to. The Penguin edition contains, as well as very full notes, an excellent Dictionary of Classical Names.

The letters

The text of Keats's letters used in these Notes is *Letters of John Keats, A selection*, edited by Robert Gittings, Oxford University Press, Oxford, 1970. The standard modern edition of all the existing letters is *The Letters of John Keats: 1814–1821*, edited by Hyder Edward Rollins, 2 vols, Harvard University Press, Cambridge, Mass., 1958.

Selections

There are three paperback editions, each of which contains a selection of poems and letters, brief notes on the text and a good critical introduction. They are:

Selected Poems and Letters of John Keats, edited by Robert Gittings, Heinemann, London, 1966. This is particularly useful as it prints the poems and extracts from the letters in chronological sequence and contains a helpful index of topics in the letters (such as 'Negative Capability' and 'Beauty and the Beautiful').

A Selection from John Keats, edited by E.C. Pettet, Longman, London, 1974. This selection also contains reproductions of some of the paintings Keats particularly admired and groups the poems under headings such as 'Joy and Sorrow', 'La Belle Dame sans Merci'. This arrangement is helpful to the study of some themes but obscures the chronological sequence of the poems and letters.

Keats: Selected Poems and Letters, edited by Roger Sharrock, Oxford
University Press, Oxford, 1964. This contains a rather shorter selec-
tion of poems and letters than the other two editions, but has an
excellent introduction.

Biography

BATE, W.J.: *John Keats*, Oxford University Press, London, 1963.
GITTINGS, ROBERT: *John Keats*, Heinemann, London, 1968, and Penguin
Books, Harmondsworth, 1979.
HILTON, TIMOTHY: *Keats and his World*, Thames & Hudson, London,
1971.
Bate's biography is a very fine, detailed study, by no means superseded
by Gittings's later version of Keats's life which contains more recently
discovered material and many challenging ideas. Hilton's book has a
short text and many illustrations of historical interest including por-
traits, maps, facsimiles of the poems in manuscript and of pages from
Keats's own books with his marginal comments.

Criticism

BATE, W.J. (ED.): *A Collection of Critical Essays*, Twentieth Century
Views, Prentice-Hall, Englewood Cliffs, N.J., 1964. A wide selec-
tion of essays with a good introduction by the editor.
BROOKS, CLEANTH: 'Keats's Sylvan Historian: History Without Foot-
notes' in *The Well Wrought Urn*, University Paperback, Methuen,
London, 1968. An interpretation of the 'Ode on a Grecian Urn'.
BUSH, DOUGLAS: *John Keats: His Life and Writings*, Collier-Macmillan,
London, 1966. A comprehensive general study.
ELIOT, T.S.: *The Use of Poetry and the Use of Criticism*, Faber, London,
1933. Contains an essay on Keats.
FOGLE, R.H.: *The Imagery of Keats and Shelley*, University of North
Carolina Press, Chapel Hill, 1949.
FRASER, G.S. (ED.): *John Keats: Odes*, Casebook Series, Macmillan,
London, 1971. A useful selection of critical essays including some by
nineteenth-century critics.
GITTINGS, ROBERT: *John Keats: The Living Year*, Heinemann, London,
1954. A detailed study of the most creative year of Keats's life, from
the autumn of 1818 to the autumn of 1819.
JACK, IAN: *Keats and the Mirror of Art*, Clarendon Press, Oxford, 1967.
A specialised study of Keats's knowledge of the visual arts, with
many illustrations.
JONES, JOHN: *John Keats's Dream of Truth*, Chatto & Windus, London,
1969. A close study of the relationship in Keats's poetry between

imagination and truth, emphasising his development from the 1817 poems onwards. A difficult but rewarding book.

LEAVIS, F.R.: 'Keats' in *Revaluation*, Chatto & Windus, London, 1936, and Penguin Books, Harmondsworth, 1972.

MATTHEWS, G.M. (ED.): *John Keats: The Critical Heritage*, Routledge & Kegan Paul, London, 1971. A selection of essays and review articles showing the changing estimation of Keats's work from first publication until 1971.

MAYHEAD, ROBIN: *John Keats*, Cambridge University Press, London, 1967. A short, clear critical study of the major poems, designed to help students whose first language is not English or who do not live in Britain.

O'NEILL, JUDITH (ED.): *Critics on Keats*, Allen & Unwin, London, 1967. A short collection of extracts from books, essays and reviews.

PETTET, E.C.: *On the Poetry of John Keats*, Cambridge University Press, London, 1957. A general study.

RICKS, CHRISTOPHER: *Keats and Embarrassment*, Oxford University Press, London, 1976. A sophisticated and stimulating exploration of the way in which Keats's moral sensibility is revealed in his poetry.

WALSH, WILLIAM: *Introduction to Keats*, Methuen, London, 1981. A short, clear discussion of the poems and the letters with particular emphasis on the development of Keats's art and sensibility.

WASSERMAN, EARL R.: *The Finer Tone*, Johns Hopkins University Press, Baltimore, Md., 1953. A detailed textual explication of five poems, 'Ode on a Grecian Urn', 'La Belle Dame Sans Merci', 'The Eve of St Agnes', 'Lamia' and 'Ode to a Nightingale'.

Keats House, Hampstead, London

Keats House was built as Wentworth Place, a pair of semi-detached houses, in 1815-16. Keats lived in both of the houses during 1818-20, the period when he wrote his greatest poetry. The 'Ode to a Nightingale' is said to have been written in the garden. The House, which is now maintained by the London Borough of Camden, is open to the public. It contains a number of rooms furnished in the style of Keats's day, and manuscripts, letters, books and other personal memorabilia of the poet and his fiancée, Fanny Brawne.

Guided tours, suitable for A level and GCSE students, can be arranged with the Curator. For further information regarding opening times, write to Keats House, Keats Grove, Hampstead, London NW3 2RR, or telephone 01 435 2062.

The author of these notes

CHARLOTTE CARSTAIRS was until 1980 a lecturer in the Department of English Language and Literature at the University of St Andrews in Scotland, where she also gained her first degree. She spent part of her childhood in the West Indies, has worked as a British Council officer in India and as a teacher of English in a secondary school in Lahore, Pakistan. In recent years she has been employed as a lecturer at the Suffolk College of Further and Higher Education in Ipswich.